Color Me Confucius

The Ethical and Moral Reset Needed for Society

William Bodri

ISBN-10: 0-9980764-8-1
ISBN-13: 978-0-9980764-8-5
Library of Congress Control Number: 2018900501

DEDICATION

To self-cultivators who wish to master the road of cultivation, and to educators who wish to teach children how to master themselves. The spiritual cultivation path that lifts us above the realm of the animals entails mastering our automatic attitudes and mental processes, and our deliberate rational thinking processes. It entails mastering control over our body, as well as control over our body's internal energy. It involves mastering the virtuous perfection of personal behavior, as well as countless other skills and talents we need for life that we can also call wisdom, conduct, behavior, activity, civilization, mastering the changes, or controlling phenomena.

The teachings of Confucius, Mencius and Wang Yang-Ming, Stoicism, Buddhism, Vedanta, Christianity, modern psychological therapies, peak achievement philosophies and more can all be combined into one great non-denominational road of spiritual progress that enables us to rise above the errant biases of our mental processes; cultivate reason, ability and virtuous action; and thereby become thoroughly human or even sagely by fully transcending our animal natures. Confucius provides many of the ground level teachings that can guide this effort of getting from here to the more ideal man and society – the Confucian way.

CONTENTS

PREFACE

The Confucian way, reinterpreted for our modern era, is almost a new philosophical school in itself. Its power lies in its ability to guide personal cultivation as well as governance policies to unify societies and larger bodies of men. The decline of ethics and morality in governments across the world requires that people look at its ethics, and start applying its methods of self-protection and self-policing to personal cultivation.

CHAPTER 1:
THE SUPREME ULTIMATE

Confucius approached the topic of spiritual cultivation in a unique way. He said we should all mindfully watch our thoughts and behavior to put ourselves on the pathway of propriety and virtue. The purpose of continually being aware of our thoughts and behavior, which you can today call mastering the state of "presence" or "awareness," is so that we can cultivate our thoughts, speech and behavior to become better people. The mindfulness of watching our thoughts helps us purify our conduct by taking it from lower animalistic tendencies to higher principles, thus divinizing it. Purifying our mind and conduct, done through mindful witnessing and ennobling, is part of the Great Learning required of life. It is the pathway to becoming a better human being, and ultimately a saint or sage.

Confucius also expected people to learn about and then be mindful of cause and effect relationships in the world. With a causal understanding of how situations come to be and how they normally develop, people can learn to guide events to more auspicious states that are better for all. Life involves learning how to improve our thoughts and behavior so that we can master events and guide them to more beneficial outcomes, especially outcomes that would improve the wellbeing of everyone. Isn't this what a saint or sage wants to accomplish?

In recognizing the importance of cause and effect, the fact we should learn from the past and stressing that we learn how to "master change" to improve situations, Confucius said that we should ultimately trace all things back to their ultimate sources. This includes situations, phenomena and

1

even our thoughts. If you understand history, for instance, you can derive common principles behind the sources of conflicts and thereby know how to avoid or change them in the future.

A true spiritual cultivator was also expected to trace his thoughts back to their origins to see why certain emotions or thoughts arose inside him. With an understanding of their roots, he could then work at untangling or purifying any of their root misconceptions. Cultivators were even expected to trace consciousness itself back to its most ultimate roots - whatever it was. For consciousness, which means thoughts and emotions, that origin was called our "inherent bright virtue," which is a mental state of pure awareness absent of thoughts yet ready to give birth to thoughts.

On a more mundane level, the meditation practice of Confucian introspection – where you constantly shine awareness on your thought processes - was developed to help people police and then uplift their thoughts and behavior. By watching your thoughts rather than getting entangled with them, in time the habit energies of unnecessary mentation will eventually die down and you will experience a more peaceful, blissful state of mind. This is how to reach the peaceful empty state of clear awareness from which thoughts arise. This is why people all over the world engage in sitting meditation practice, which is so that they can eventually realize their inherently bright virtue – the pristine pure awareness of consciousness that separates us from insentience.

Mencius added that the process of spiritual cultivation also involved cultivating your Qi or vitality, which is something you should do on a daily basis. Thus, a Confucian was to cultivate both his mind to a state of purity (where it became so clear that an individual could know his own thoughts with clarity and without losing himself) and his internal energy that permeated and composed his body.

Confucius relied on the *Yijing* for his worldview of phenomena and the metaphysical order. The *Yijing*, which therefore represents views that we should reference to unravel Confucianism, enters into the transcendental and material spheres. It states that the entire universe comes from Taiji (Tai Qi), which is an fundamental Supreme Ultimate – an original nature.

The Supreme Ultimate stands for the foundational essence, energy or absolute nature that transcends all subsequently created, manifest, conditioned phenomena of the universe. It is the single, pure primordial origin of the universe spoken of by philosophers. It is the Great Tao of

Taoism, Parabrahman of Hinduism, original nature of Buddhism, Allah of Islam, Ein Sof of Judaism and God the Father of Christianity.

The Supreme Ultimate is the absolute origin of the universe of created things. It is like one pure energy from which all other energies and matter are derived, and being the most fundamental existence before all else is self-so, uncreated, self-sufficient, infinite, eternal, unchangeable. Being the origin in a state of aloneness it is single, pure, ultimate, self-born. Unmanifest into anything else due to changelessness, yet it is the single foundational base that has produced infinite variations of manifestation within itself. It is the single, non-dual, undifferentiated supreme essence of all existence that transcends all created phenomenal things since they are evolutes from its single nature and appear within it. As simply an energy or essence or foundational state, within it there is no knowingness and no consciousness because such things are constructions. There is only itself.

Basically there is nothing prior to the Supreme Ultimate in existence or beingness. It is not a living being, but it is the root source of all things, the primal essence from which everything arises and which nothing can possibly transcend. Like space it has no divisions or secondary characteristics.

As the ultimate original energy that has developed into an infinitude of others, it is a purity that transcends all composite forms, phenomena, conditions and appearances. It transcends all forces and matter and creations including consciousness, which is a construction arising within matter. Consciousness arises within living beings structured in a certain way and animated by energy. It is just a product of the right causes and conditions. The Supreme Ultimate is the ultimate source of all life and consciousness that have somehow formed/evolved/appeared within it.

When any living creature says "I" it actually refers to this underlying essence, the true self of the Supreme Ultimate that is the common self (nature) of all things. When anyone says "I" it is in truth the self-nature announcing itself. Besides the fact that "I" points to the individual, every living being saying "I" is actually referring to the common single source essence that comprises the entire universe - the Supreme Ultimate.

The Supreme Ultimate becomes many forms or bodies; all the many phenomenal worlds in the universe arise and subside within it while it doesn't change. Being the Supreme Essence at their foundational nature, every living being can rightfully say, "They are all me. Every existence is my existence, every consciousness is my consciousness for I am just the original essence." In other words, the total functioning and appearance of the universe is just *you* because you are ultimately the Source Essence or Supreme Ultimate. All beings are therefore your brothers and sisters.

The Supreme Ultimate was never born and will never die, so you (because you are that energy) were never born and will never die. Exist or not exist as an individual you are still here always. As the Supreme Ultimate existed before consciousness appeared, because you are this foundational essence you were there before consciousness appeared. Through logic you can realize that your body, your vital energy and even the consciousness in you in their utmost pristine purity are all the Supreme Ultimate. The consciousness of you and every other being as well as matter find their ultimate unity and identity in the Supreme Ultimate, or original nature.

The objective of Confucianism, in tracing all things back to their ultimate source, includes helping you reach an experience of an "empty," clear, pristine or pure state of mind that resembles the Supreme Ultimate, which is called cultivating your bright virtue. For instance, what transcends thoughts is the natural mind that is there before their appearance - a state of consciousness that is alive and aware but absent of thoughts. What is there is a state where thoughts are unborn but their birth is not suppressed. This state of purity and clarity is to be considered as "pure consciousness" or "pristine" awareness. This is your bright virtue, namely the ability to form thoughts out of seemingly nothingness or emptiness because you have sentience or awareness. Like the Supreme Ultimate that is itself empty of all other things, like space, your natural mind is empty of thoughts but like the Supreme Ultimate can also give birth to all things – thoughts and emotions arise and depart within it according to conditions.

Our mental bright virtue is a pristine awareness absent of thoughts ready to know whatever appears rather than an inert absence of thoughts (thoughtlessness) equivalent to insentience or the lethargic ignorance of sleep. This clarity of perception is what you are to cultivate as Confucian practice, and is called empty mind in Buddhism, pure awareness in Vedanta or just bright mind.

Your mind should be comfortably quiet and aware but not suppressing thoughts. You must always allow thoughts to arise and when they are born (appear) you should clearly know them and manipulate them with skillfulness as necessary. You should always "know your mind" or "know your thoughts," but you don't have to act on everything that arises within your head. Some thoughts need to be ignored. You should know what you are thinking and why, but you should not get so entangled with your thoughts and emotions that they totally possess you and you fall into confusion. Rather, you have to develop the mental skill of standing apart from them so you can evaluate them with wisdom and transcend their pulls. The goal is to become their total master so that you can use them skillfully or ignore them as you like.

In Confucianism you are to cultivate a bright state of being where your mind is clear like a cloudless sky and your thoughts are always known with clarity. Because you do not cling to them they are like birds flying across the sky that leave no trace of their passage. This fully aware brightness of being is the state of conscious aliveness. It is called a state of bliss, serenity, peace or calmness but it is really just equanimous peaceful awareness, which is the natural state of your mind.

Inertness is not the ultimate state of existence because the Supreme Ultimate somehow gives birth to the cosmos without itself changing, and therefore no-thought, not knowing, confusion or ignorance are not the ideal states of a sentient being. We are to know things and master them.

A person following the Confucian path should cultivate in an analogous fashion to the Supreme Ultimate that has all things arise within it that operate according to laws of cause and effect. We are to know them. The base or foundational state of the mind should always remains clear and pure like an empty sky or the Supreme Ultimate, but consciousness should always allow all thoughts to arise within it without attachments or rejection just as the Supreme Ultimate allows all phenomena to appear.

All the things that arise in the mind are just creations of consciousness just as all things in the universe are the creations of the Supreme Ultimate. In the sense that thoughts reflect a world they are true, but in the sense that they are not absolutes but just conditional imperfect reflections they are false. Everything that arises within the mind is a form of consciousness layered with emotional likes and dislikes that distort the already imperfect images, but to make correct decisions and rise to the heights of correct thinking one has to put aside these emotional biases and navigate their thoughts using wisdom.

In Hinduism it is taught that the purity of empty consciousness and the thoughts that arise within it are like the union of Shiva (the Supreme

Ultimate that never moves or changes like space) and Shakti (the scintillating universe of matter and energy in constant change and motion). Once again, this is the model of correct spiritual cultivation. Your mind at rest must become empty and clear like the pure and stainless Supreme Ultimate, but must also allow thoughts to arise within it and you must know them or you are insentient. For humans the external realm of conquest is the universe of matter and energy whereas the internal realm to be conquered involves your thoughts. It is not only the natural world we must master. You must learn how to control/use your thoughts, which is akin to "guiding the changes" as instructed by the *Yijing*, so that you can use them to investigate matters, solve problems, and guide your conduct to always create the best state of affairs.

The ultimate aim of Confucianism is that you elevate yourself to transcendence or sagehood, which requires mastery of these principles in application. The pathway requires that you must understand the nature of the Supreme Ultimate, which is the unchanging, pure, ultimate source of all things. Then you have to cultivate your mind's awareness so that it operates in an analogous fashion.

You absolutely can achieve this through a self-perfection pathway of spiritual cultivation. The pathway is to practice witnessing the workings of your consciousness until they calm down, clarify, and then the empty but perfectly free nature of clear awareness – your natural mind - can be directly experienced. This is called emptiness, purity, base consciousness or pure awareness. The Confucian way is to use meditation and mental watching to continually cultivate a pure mind of base awareness, proper thinking and virtuous behavior until they all reach the highest standards of excellence.

Within the perfect clarity of mental knowing your thoughts will always arise, and you should always know them clearly (which is another meaning of "tracing things to their source"), understand what they indicate, and comprehend the cause and effect of what they will probably lead to. In knowing one's thoughts and circumstances, a person can learn to perfect their behavior and master situations, and in this way becomes a sage.

Additionally, because the Supreme Ultimate is pure, your thoughts and behavior must also ultimately become pure in terms of virtuousness and morality, which are the highest states of humanity and divinity. This is the road of Confucian cultivation.

CHAPTER 2:
THE MANIFEST UNIVERSE

How does Confucius characterize the manifest universe that
Buddhism calls the Triple Realm, Hinduism calls Shakti or Prakirti, Taoism
calls the Cosmos, and Christianity calls Creation or the Kingdom of the
Father?

Confucianism speaks of the manifest universe as "Nature" or the *union
of Heaven and Earth*. Everything in existence appears as the union of Heaven
and Earth where Heaven and Earth stand as opposites. Earth stands for the
planet earth as well as the manifest realm of solidity and appearance.
Heaven stands not just for the vast heavenly cosmos of empty space and
the invisible spiritual reality of gods and deities, but also other unseen or
unfathomable forces that create and order the cosmos.

In its ultimate aspect Heaven stands for the unmoving, unchangeable
source essence or Supreme Ultimate – the original nature whose sublimity is
often referred to as an emptiness or void in Buddhism (or formlessness in
Vedanta) due to its purity of not being composed of anything else. This is
the Purusha (or Shiva) of Hinduism, Parabrahman of Vedanta, the original
nature of Buddhism, the Ein Sof of Judaism, Allah of Islam and the
Heavenly Father of Christianity. The ultimate essence of your physical body
is also *This* at the utmost root and in the Yoga schools of India you are
taught to cultivate the constituent components of your body back to more
primordial energies, and then ultimately *This*.

Heaven is vast, and all things appear within it. All of Creation falls
within its vast space just as all things fall within the Supreme Ultimate.

Looking up at the skies, all things *do appear or manifest* within Heaven including the Earth. The Earth doesn't just stand for the earthly globe or solid matter but for the tangible reality of the manifest universe. It all appears within space, meaning Heaven. It also all appears within the original nature, the Supreme Ultimate or primordial essence.

Matter and motion stands for Shakti, the manifestation or Creation that appears within the Supreme Ultimate (represented by Heaven). Manifestation does not have to assume the status of solidity (for instance magnetism is a manifestation), but is something that is different from the purity of the original energy. It is some type of derivative product. Evolutes (manifestations) must be considered emanations or condensations derived from the original essence through myriads of complex transformations.

Mencius said, "the union of Heaven and Earth gives birth to all things" and "Heaven and Earth are the origins of life." In other words, Shiva and Shakti, Prakirti and Purusha, Nirguna Brahman (without attributes) and Saguna Brahman (with attributes), the original nature and its evolutes, the absolute essence and the Triple Realm, the Supreme Ultimate and Manifestation together produce all things. The two opposites interpenetrate; the always moving manifestation is within the unmoving changeless Supreme Ultimate (symbolized by the vast emptiness of Heaven) and the Supreme Ultimate permeates all Creation as their source essence substance. Everything together must be considered as melded into one single whole with nothing existent outside the ultimate oneness. Cultivation schools use this analogy to point out that thoughts appear within the purity of consciousness that seems to be an emptiness, stillness, formlessness, voidness or no-thought.

Through cause and effect the origins of life and consciousness can be traced back to more fundamental universal forces. The ultimate root source or end point of all those trace-backs is the singular Supreme Ultimate, the purest source energy/substance of everything. Because of cause and effect ruling all things we can be sure that consciousness, or life, appears as a result of prior forces too even though with modern science we cannot yet trace it back to its ultimate origins. Its production is simply described as a result of the union of Heaven and Earth within Confucianism.

To reach the enlightenment of a sage you must transcend any habit energy of clinging to your thoughts so that you imitate the nature of the Supreme Ultimate, or original nature, that never moves like space yet lets everything freely appear within it without clinging to anything. This is why a Confucian practitioner aligns themselves as the witness or observer who watches their thoughts that are always changing within a base of seemingly pure, unmoving clarity – the pristine empty awareness of the mind, its bright virtue.

The fundamental method of Confucian cultivation is to mindfully watch, witness or observe your thoughts and behavior in all you do in order to develop clarity and self-correction. Your awareness never interferes with your thoughts just as the Supreme Ultimate never interferes with Shakti, its emanations of Creation, and yet the Supreme Ultimate is manifest in everything because it is their source essence or foundational energy. It interpenetrates everything like space and so you must come to recognize that your thoughts (which are the only things you know) are consciousness, and the world you see is just your consciousness-only too.

Confucianism is no different than other great spiritual traditions in emphasizing that what characterizes the manifest universe is constant change. Everything around you is always experiencing a continual state of transformation. This fact has implications for how to manage your mind and behavior. In life we are to learn how to master or guide these changes just as we are to learn how to master and guide our thoughts.

Inherent, incessant change is the dynamic inherent in the universe that qualifies every one of its manifestations. The implication of constant change is that we should avoid strong attachment to thoughts, such as afflictions, that naturally arise in our minds because they will change. That is their destiny. We tend to hold onto them but they are not meant to stay in our minds except during the process of concentration. For instance, we should not hold onto mental afflictions and rehash them.

Furthermore, just as we should not hold onto errant or afflictive thoughts or wrong emotions when inappropriate we should prevent society from becoming ossified by inflexible social rules and structures, which mistakenly happened to Confucianists in the past. Religious rules, ritualistic (traditional) expectations, social obligations and so forth should never become so inflexible and encumbering that people find their country or culture claustrophobic and oppressive. No one wants to be micromanaged by inflexible, unchanging rules and expectations – from either the government, society or religion – that end up turning life into a psychic prison. This outcome is wrong as well as an errant interpretation of the proper application of Confucianism.

The dynamism of the manifest universe is called "transformation" in Taoism, "impermanence" in Buddhism, "change" in Confucianism, "Shakti" (movement) in Hinduism and "complex interaction" in Islam. Ceaseless transformation is a primary characteristic of the cosmos and the reason that one is told not to attach to mental thoughts on the road of self-cultivation, for why should you cling to something that naturally changes every moment and is destined to leave? Because change is immanently inherent in situations, this principle should also give us hope that we can change unfortunate situations into something better, which is the Confucian ideal of improvement by managing changes. The Confucian ideal is to learn how to manage change to bring about better states of existence.

While the Confucian Shao Yung refers to the words "change" and "mutation" to denote the alternations characterizing the phenomena of the universe, the term "*sheng sheng*" (production and reproduction) is also commonly used in Confucian and Neo-Confucian texts to indicate the ongoing process of incessant change that characterizes manifest reality. As with Taoism, Confucianism clearly recognizes that the complex interactions within the infinite web of the universe are an on-going process of ceaseless transformation.

The major theme of the *Yijing*, central to Confucianism, is continuous creative change. Confucius said, "with vitality and endurance Heaven acts without ceasing! Heaven's motion is the healthiest." In Confucianism, Taoism and Chinese culture in general, this change or motion is said to be brought about by two polar forces of yin (passivity, rest or non-movement) and yang (activity or change) perpetually interacting to generate the universe.

Buddhism uses the terms "birth and death" to describe the endless process of change while Hinduism uses the trio of appearance-production, preservation-duration, and cessation- dissolution to signify the same thing. These are symbolized by Brahma the Creator, Vishnu the Preserver and Shiva the Destroyer. Western science simply talks about interactions, evolution or transformations when it talks of change. All major religions agree that the changeful nature of manifest creations means that all phenomena are unstable, existing like ungraspable illusions as contrasted with the unchanging Supreme Ultimate, which is unmoving like space.

Why all this emphasis on change and stationarity? So what?

The reason for the emphasis is as follows. Confucianism explains that we must accept change as a natural part of the cosmos. We should learn to be flexible rather than fixed and rigid. We must inquire and research and adapt ourselves rather than let things stay constant. Human beings should "model themselves on the ceaseless vitality of the cosmic processes."

Although change characterizes the manifest universe and the unseen forces that produce man and phenomena, because things are interconnected we can learn how to master the changes in an active fashion to produce better states of the future. We absolutely must learn how to properly manage and master change, for this is what leads to progress and freedom from lower states of existence.

This emphasis is one of the highlights of Confucianism, which extends from the idea of mastering oneself to also mastering "others" such as situations and phenomena. One can and should learn how to both accept and manage the changes of life and circumstances, bringing all to more favorable positions. This does not mean fighting against the ceaseless vitality of the cosmic processes, but using and managing processes for specific purposes of betterment.

This attitude is especially useful for when we encounter obstacles and difficulties in our lives. We need to persevere through hardship with strength of will and quiet determination while we try to change negative circumstances for the better. We must work on bettering our own positions as well as improving the greater world. In particular, our actions should be appropriate for any situation, as well as be in accord with proper timing and circumstances. In strategy, a Confucian always makes use of opportune timing and circumstances to accomplish more using less.

Taoists also believe that we should harmonize our actions to be in tune with universal changes, whether they be of the seasons, phenomena, relationships, and so on, so that we are not fighting forces stronger than ourselves. Confucianism insists that the human processes which develop society, especially the relationships between people, should also be in harmonious accord with one another. People need to learn their role in the network of relationships that define a family or community and thereby fulfill behaviors that maintain peaceful social harmony. In other words, people need to know their duties and responsibilities within families and society such as the proper way of behaving toward others and how *not to be errant*. By acting in accord with these norms, one produces a cooperative, cohesive society which can act as a thriving whole. This mirrors the fact that all things are interconnected in one whole because they ultimately share the same ultimate Supreme Nature.

In *Inquiry on the Great Learning* the Confucian master Wang Yang-Ming said, "The great man regards Heaven and Earth and the myriad of things as one body. He regards the world as one family and the country as one person. As to those who make a cleavage between objects and distinguish between the self and others, they are small men. That the great man can regard Heaven, Earth and the myriad of things as one body is not because he deliberately wants to do so, but because it is nature to the humane nature of his mind that he do so. ... Everything from the ruler, minister, husband, wife, and friends to mountains, rivers, spiritual beings, birds, animals, and plants should be truly loved in order to realize my humanity that forms one body with them, and then my clear character will be completely manifested, and I really form one body with Heaven, Earth and the myriad of things."[1]

Wang Yang-Ming also said, "Heaven and earth are one structure with me; spirits and gods are in one all-pervading unity with me." Again, "Man is the mind of Heaven and Earth. Heaven, Earth and the ten thousand things form originally a unity with me." He also said, "Man is only separated from Heaven and Earth by his body."

Thus man must cultivate not just his mind but also his body to become one with the Tao. Confucianism offers some pointers on this, but for better guidance on this aspect of the Confucian way we should turn to Yoga, Taoism and Buddhist Vajrayana.

---

[1] Wing-Tsit Chan, *A Source Book in Chinese Philosophy* (Princeton University Press, Princeton, 1969).

CHAPTER 3:
THE PROCESS OF UNIVERSAL CREATION

According to the *Yijing*, the manifest universe appears due to the evolution of yin and yang forces that originate from the Supreme Ultimate. These energies somehow develop out of the single absolute essence that is so pure and alone in itself that it is considered undifferentiated or without attributes (since any secondary characteristics you could identify would already be admitting of a second essence). Thus the Supreme Ultimate is therefore often compared to a great emptiness like space to denote its absolute purity. Incomprehensible, it is often used as a subject of meditation to help people free their minds of thoughts. They are taught to let their minds be pure and empty just like It, the Supreme Utimate.

The *Yijing* does not say how the changeless Supreme Ultimate, a solitary existence transcending everything created, produces the dualities of yin and yang. It does not say how forces developed from a supreme Oneness that is simply one single unchanging essence that permeates/is the whole of existence, and unable to evolve into anything else since it is the primal and only (sole) existent essence.

This mystery of manifestation in Buddhism is called "Ignorance," which means "we do not know how" the unmoving, pure, changeless absolute nature gives birth to the first formational (karmic) forces of the created manifest universe – we are *ignorant* of the process. Some Hindu schools suggest that a perturbation or stirring arises within the Supreme Ultimate that ends up kick starting Creation, but once again no one can say how. Nevertheless, according to the *Yijing* the Ultimate One gives birth to the dualities of yin and yang forces and then the rest of the universe, eventually including myriad forms of life. With life comes consciousness, so consciousness is born within matter from the complex interaction or evolutionary development of all these forces. It is an evolutionary or transformational consequence of a large set or long sequence of prior cause and effect interactions. Who knows what life will lead to, but we can certainly learn to guide its changes.

In the *Yijing* the Supreme Ultimate stands for our absolute nature, which is the "fundamental essence" or "original nature" of Zen Buddhism. As stated, the Supreme Ultimate is that primal energy from which existence somehow flows (being itself the only unchanging and thus *real* existence), but no one can say how the flow begins since the pure Ultimate without contamination (The One Without a Second) is pure, changeless, motionless, and eternal. The *Yijing* only states that there is a constant alternation of forces in the *manifested* universe, such as yin and yang, that through interactions evolutionarily produce the five elements and then the entire universe from there. The prepositional support of all universal forces is the Supreme Ultimate, which is therefore their ground state, Mother source, fundamental essence or truest nature that is inseparable from their own existence, permeating them with the support of its own self-so existence.

The creation of yin and yang, which is a foundational principle within Chinese philosophy and culture, is simply an analogy for the creation of energy, karmic forces, creational energies or foundational forces in the universe from which everything else is developed. It is through their mutual interactions, with forces fundamentally interpenetrating and mutually producing each other, that all matter is somehow developed in transformations.

The *Yijing* basically incorporates the foundational notions of creativity and change within the two concepts of yin and yang said to characterize all processes and relationships. Through two fundamental forces of yin and yang, which develop into other forces via transformations, changes, interactions or evolutions, it provides a theory of manifest reality, how it came about and how to interpret it or guide it.

Thus the yin and yang of the *Yijing* are just Chinese names for the foundational, formational forces of the universe (Creation) and their interactions. They don't stand for two forces but for many forces. For instance, according to the *Yijing* symbolism used to explain the evolution of

Creation, the two primal yin and yang forces differentiate into four phenomena (images) or forces named Lesser Yin, Great Yin, Lesser Yang and Great Yang. These four forces then intermingle to become the eight trigrams (*Bagua*) that then produce sixty-four forces symbolized by hexagrams of the *Yijing*. Hence, yin and yang actually represent innumerable forces other than just two.

All of these evolutions of yin and yang symbolize forces being composed of more primal components, and those components are composed of even more primal components still. An equivalence in matter is that solid objects are composed of atoms that are composed of electrons, protons and neutrons, which are in turn composed of quarks and gluons, and so on. Eventually at the end of this chain of causality you arrive at the singular Supreme Ultimate or foundational energy that cannot be further subdivided. Therefore it must have been the self-existing self-so beginning. But how the oneness, purity or singleness of the Supreme Ultimate can generate another thing within itself different from its solitary pureness (since it allows no change in its purity of being) is a great quandary.

Nevertheless, there is in the *Yijing* the Great Primal Beginning that generates the two primary forces that then generate the four images (phenomena). The four images generate the eight trigrams that determine good fortune and misfortune (phenomena) and so on. As the *Yijing* further states, good fortune and misfortune create the field of action.

Forget about whether yin and yang become four forces, or five, or eight or nine or whatever. You have to grasp the symbolism being communicated. The *Yijing's* philosophical principle is that essences, substances, forces, energies or phenomena develop into other things through an interdependence of cause and effect expressed within evolutionary transformations.

The distinctions and transformations of yin and yang are said to produce the five elements of the universe, which is another way of analyzing its components into more primal forces. Once again, all of these symbolic schemes are simply representative of forces being composed of higher, more transcendental forces, and those forces or energies are composed of yet higher transcendental forces still. At the end of the stream of tracing things back you end up with one single energy or force that the *Yijing* calls the Supreme Ultimate. Other schools call it Parabrahman, the original nature, Allah, Ein Sof and so on as previously stated. Starting from this one Supreme Ultimate you somehow generate firmer/denser (more condensed) spheres or realms of existence/energy, and looking upwards from the densest sphere of energy (ours) we say you get transcendental spheres or purer realms of essences/energies above us.

Thus in Chinese culture the material world is transcended by the spiritual world of Qi, which is transcended by a higher spiritual world composed of Shen, which is composed of a yet higher spiritual world composed of Later Heavenly energy, which is composed of yet higher forces composed of Primordial Heavenly energy. According to the *Yijing* (as well as Buddhism), all these various forces, energies and realms interpenetrate. They all simultaneously co-exist within each other and through perfect interpenetration comprise one whole. They are integrated into one single body by their interrelationships that involve them in an endless cycle of production and reproduction. Nothing exists independently of this whole because it is all interconnected. The Confucian Zhang Zai aptly said, the sage "forms one body with the universe."

According to Confucianism, Nature is to be seen as a unified, interconnected, and interpenetrating whole of constantly self-generating interrelations of higher and lower forces. This is similar to the *Hua-Yen* viewpoint of Buddhism where the universe is like a great chain of being, an infinite net of interrelationships in a container or womb where each individual phenomenon is in a continual process of transformation that involves and links all other life, matter and forces. No single thing is a substantial, independent thing but rather is a conditional creation whose existence is dependent upon everything else. Everything is linked in a single whole, so each part within the whole is interdependent with all others. Buddhism therefore says that all things are fundamentally "empty," with "empty" meaning that *they do not exist independently* (because they don't) and are impermanent since they don't endure. The are "empty" of real existence that doesn't change since they are transient existences. The *real* is what stays and endures changelessly so being impermanent they are disqualified from being real. They are "empty of true reality." Only the original nature, the changeless Supreme Ultimate, merits the title of being *real*.

Each part of the cosmos is therefore like a drop of water in the great ocean that is inseparable from the greater ocean due to interdependence and by virtue of being in the ocean is linked with all its other drops. Every part is simultaneously both a drop *and* the entire ocean, with the analogy that every part of the cosmos is fundamentally a part and the whole universe. When in the ocean a drop is but the ocean itself, and only separated from the ocean does it become a drop. In the universe there is no way to separate anything from itself to become independent since the universe defines every thing through massive, inconceivable, infinite interdependence. Thus there is no such thing as a drop, thing, entity, life, ego, force, energy, substance, phenomenon, etc. that exists by itself separate from the Supreme Ultimate for everything is ultimately bound together, and thus everything (all phenomena and conditions) works together to define even the tiniest phenomenon. The universe is thus seen in a single atom.

The billions of drops which comprise the ocean do not have any consciousness, so as phenomena they do not know that they are drops, nor that they are in the ocean, nor that they are part of the ocean, nor that the ocean even exists. Insentience is the original state of changeless Reality and its manifestation of phenomena. It is just a wondrous miracle that sentient consciousness has somehow developed within the womb of the insentient Universe. How consciousness has formed via evolution no one knows. We only know that life has evolved out of matter and consciousness out of life, and we are conscious biological mechanisms within this Great Ultimate. We are also impermanent temporary phenomena, the result of the accumulated effects of countless past causes and conditions.

What is important to know is that like the drops of water in the ocean we are intimately bound up with one another such that the burdens and benefits of others are also ours through the interdependence or interpenetration of existence. For instance, if someone altruistically creates benefit for others then they benefit, and we do too. We all share in the benefits from the aggregate strivings of others creating the world and environment in which we live. We can, through our individual actions, therefore make the world a better or worse place in which to live because the world is created through the composite efforts of all human beings. No matter how small or insignificant you feel is your contribution, the world is created by summing together all such contributions, so your efforts count. Are you therefore making the world a better place, or making it worse off through your actions and behavior? Confucius asked us to pursue virtuous ways to make it better.

One can say about each and every phenomena in the universe that everything actually is just the Supreme Ultimate, everything is from the

Supreme Ultimate, everything is permeated by the Supreme Ultimate, and everything is in the Supreme Ultimate. Everything is a manifestation or evolute of the Supreme Ultimate foundational energy or essence, and no single thing has been created for any particular reason. Every phenomenon that exists has happened to become created as a result of matter and energy interacting and transforming according to the laws of nature that have developed. We, like everything else in the universe, are also just phenomena created without any particular reason, but we are one of the phenomena that has consciousness. In particular we are animals, and as animals the spiritual path for us - whatever we might argue it to be - should involve cultivating our consciousness. We should cultivate both our reasoning abilities and actions/behavior to produce better states of being for ourselves and others. This is the spiritual path.

Within this whole matrix of Creation the *Yijing* poses no Creator God because the universe is simply a self-generating process, contained within itself, whose ultimate support or foundation is the absolute *Taiji*, the Supreme Ultimate or highest nature that is simply a single solitary essence without any intentional purpose. It is neutral. We are the ones who must therefore choose a purpose for our lives. How could this ultimate unchanging essence or energy – the highest purest One – ever be a being, person, entity or life with a purpose? And also, what is the Universe evolving to in terms of a purpose since things are simply happening?

Since there is no ultimate Creator God and no ultimate intended purpose to Creation and what it is evolving into, in Confucianism *you must become the creator of your own life and the manager responsible for developing your own destiny through wisdom!* This is why you need to learn how to master the changes of phenomena, including the complexities of human situations. Man must learn how to "master the changes" so that he can make things better, recreating the world after the ideals he chooses. The idea of responding to the world and creating appropriate institutions, laws or solutions to problems is another example of "mastering the changes."

Within this scintillating whole, a true Confucian must learn how to guide situations and circumstances to states of prosperous cooperation and how to also be in harmony with all states, interactions or relationships he encounters. He must learn how to control himself and adjust himself to the forces that affect him and how to change or guide those forces to something better. Because man is a self-conscious individual who can use intelligence, his capability for being able to guide changes should be viewed as part of his ideal character. Developing his mental and behavioral skills to the fullest is what helps to separate man from the animals and rise above them by creating culture and life purpose where there is none. This is part of the spiritual path for life.

How to "master your mental processes" and "guide the changes" is therefore what one should strive to master in life, and is the basis of the teachings of the *Yijing*. The *Yijing* clearly stresses that one of your highest capabilities is learning how to "master the changes" of phenomena in order to bring about whatever you want. Confucianism teaches how to do this in regards to yourself. Because your mind can do this it is the wish-fulfilling gem of Buddhism.

The best transformations you can create are those that promote the positive, namely harmonious prosperity and auspiciousness for all. This includes the harmonious growth and development of individuals, communities, societies and the world. Since few actions are perfectly good, pragmatism suggests that we shouldn't bemoan the fact that no actions are perfect when we try to achieve such objectives but nevertheless our actions should accent the good in the greatest degree possible.

No sun exists without sunspots just as there is no such thing as perfectly empty space or perfect pure yin or yang. No fish can live in the perfect purity of distilled water either. Therefore no action you take in the world can be perfectly good, for we can always find some minor flaw in it. Because nothing is perfectly good, the rule is that we should maximally lean towards the good in all our dealings. That's the best you can do.

This is called skillful means, which means accepting that errors will always accompany whatever we try to do in life and that it is almost impossible to be perfectly pure, so you just have to act with maximum skillfulness. Nevertheless there is still the ideal of perfect behavior, which Confucius indicated is to "act without making serious mistakes." The practical ideal is to maximally lean towards the good in all that you do. In Confucianism this is called exemplary action or "consummate conduct."

Wang Yang-Ming taught that cultivating personal morality was the way that individuals within society could create social well-being. Along these lines, Confucius said that ordering the world ultimately started with self-cultivation, meaning that it started with everyone adopting the personal aim of perfecting their own self behavior. He felt you must cultivate yourself and develop strong moral bearings before you can truly succeed in bringing about beneficial change in the world. Positive change must start with individuals, meaning *you*. In addition to tracing the mind back to its ultimate source – the Supreme Ultimate Essence - the road of self-cultivation towards better thought and behavior is a critical part of the great road of Confucian cultivation. It is the heart of the Confucian way.

Wang Yang-Ming said, "Man is only separated from Heaven and Earth by his body," which means that he must not just purify his thoughts and behavior but also transform his body so that it more easily becomes something reflecting the unity of Heaven and Earth. By working the chain of causation backwards, logically the first stage of transformation is for the matter of the body to be purified into Qi, Qi into the more transcendental Shen, Shen into Later Heavenly Qi and Later Heavenly Qi into Primordial Heavenly Qi. Can man really attain a body composed of such purified transcendence? If so, that road must start with the purification of your Qi. This is a pathway explained in Yoga, Taoism, Buddhism and many other spiritual schools across the world which state that the proposed ideal is not just hearsay but something doable.

Mencius once said that he was good at nurturing his vast and overflowing Qi that is, in the highest degree, unlimited and unmoving. He said, "If it is nourished with integrity and is not injured, it will fill the space between Heaven and Earth. This Qi is the companion [produced by] of rightness and the Way; without rightness and the Way, this Qi will starve. It is born from an accumulation of rightness and not an occasional show of rightness. Action that is below the standard set in one's mind will starve the Qi." In other words, performing virtuous actions is one way of transforming your Qi, and this can help kick off this set of Qi transformations. The purification of your Qi is part of the transformations required for producing a sage, and the purification of Qi has to do with your behavior.

On the road of cultivation to become a sage, you must be clear that you need to cultivate both your thoughts/mind and your Qi, your behavior and your body. Sages rarely stress this, but cultivation is a mind-body affair that requires you to purify your mind, behavior and your Qi through ardent cultivation efforts.

CHAPTER 4:
THE CONFUCIAN STAGES
OF MENTAL PRACTICE

Confucius referred to enlightenment as finding one's "bright virtue." In *The Great Learning* he said that discovering and expressing one's bright virtue should be the foremost goal in life for all human beings. Everyone, from the Emperor down to the common man without exception, should be cultivating throughout his life in order to become enlightened as to their bright virtue. This is a mind-body achievement that entails the search to discover the clear awareness of your mind, its many functional capabilities, its ability to become purified, and its ability to generate altruistic, virtuous, pure behavior.

Thus the search for one's bright virtue not only represents personal perfection in thought, word and deed but the act of finding the pristine fundamental essence of your mind, which is the clarity of awareness that allows you to know. Since knowing our minds (thoughts) clearly separates us from the animals and elevates us, self-cultivation along these lines is to be regarded as the foundation of transcendental training.

"Bright virtue" refers to the clear aspect of consciousness, which we can match in an comparable manner with the pure source nature of the universe that is pristine and empty of all other things - like space. We can also call it pure consciousness or pristine awareness. This is the clear light of Tibetan Buddhism, pure awareness of Vedanta, the uncreated light of Christianity, and so on. It is the light of awareness of the mind that is there before any appearance of knowledge. It isn't a substance, but simply a state of consciousness ready to know while thoughts are in abeyance. It is our ability to know things. Pristine, clear, bright awareness is your bright virtue. It is your miraculous ability to know things, namely ready consciousness.

Confucius described the cultivation pathway to recognizing your bright virtue as composed of seven steps. While his description is more simplistic than the details found in some traditions such as Buddhism, it adequately guides you through the cultivation path in broad strokes.

According to Confucius's teachings, the first stage of the spiritual path is (1) cultivating **awareness**. Anyone who is practicing a spiritual path in some genuine tradition always starts out by being told to be good and refrain from evil ways. They are taught that they should watch their thoughts so that they always know what they are and can therefore police themselves to do good and avoid evil. Through the awareness of self-observation you should know your intentions clearly, which is "practicing awareness," and through awareness you can police your actions so that they reflect a better human nature.

You cannot change what you are unaware of, so the first stage of spiritual paths everywhere is an emphasis on awareness. Instructions are given in many religions such as "you need to turn away from evil ways that you were previously following and now turn toward the light." Basically we need to become more aware of what we are thinking, saying or doing and intending in order to gain control over our behavior and move it towards goodness.

Whether Christian or Jew, Moslem, Hindu, Buddhist or Confucian, everyone starts out upon the spiritual path by practicing awareness (mental watching or observation) to police their attitudes, thoughts and behavior. The best way to master this skill to a degree of excellence is by practicing witnessing meditation on a regular basis, and mindfulness during non-meditative periods, until the habit of observing your thoughts - rather than getting hopelessly entangled in them such as by getting transfixed by emotional attachments - becomes consistent everywhere. Witnessing meditation and mindfulness of your thoughts helps you develop a detached, independent perspective of your thoughts, which are to be seen as potentially useful objects of your mind to be manipulated rather than absolutely true realities.

Through awareness you can clearly know what you are thinking and doing in the presence of *now* and then immediately correct any errors you observe in your mental logic, words and behaviors. Cultivating clear awareness of how things are is the first step towards improving any situation, including your fate and fortune. Furthermore, the practice of continually shining awareness on your own mental realm to know/observe your thoughts and what you are doing will at the very minimum end up making you a better person when you use this for self-correction.

This is practicing the Confucian way, which makes you more self-aware and able to reach greater benefits in life due to increased awareness. At a higher stage of practice it will eventually open up all your Qi channels so that you become healthier and live longer. At the maximum level of achievement it will lead to Qi transformations that let you enter the spiritual realms. However, no one can attain the highest of spiritual stages unless they cultivate being a virtuous person.

From the practice of mindful mental introspection (called "mindfulness" in Buddhism and "awareness" in Vedanta) to correct your behavior you will end up becoming a happier and better person than you would have been had you not adopted the practice. This is because you will become knowledgeable about faults and errors when they occur, and will then be able to cut them off at the moment of recognition. This stopping will allow you to better master situations, as is taught by the *Yijing*, because you can prevent yourself from going too far. In the light of "mastering the changes" once again, it will allow you improve your fortune and destiny. Better said, it will change your human fortune and destiny for the better. By cultivating a clear present awareness of what you are actually thinking, saying and doing and learning how to cut off what is errant so as to correct yourself, you will thereby cultivate the single most powerful tool in the universe towards becoming a better human being – your mind.

In the western school of Christianity this is called cultivating virtue while in Confucianism it is phrased in terms of ethics, morality, propriety and consummate behavior. It is the pathway to becoming a more virtuous, human being who transcends the ordinary way of unthinking men who often cannot control themselves. While the road of Confucian cultivation always involves rectifying your mind, when describing it people usually refer to its emphasis on positive behavior. The point is that virtue, or positive behavior, *cannot be achieved without cultivating awareness* so Confucius stressed that the first step of the spiritual path should be to cultivate greater awareness of the workings and contents of your mind.

By continual mindfulness in cultivating an awareness of your mental realm and your behavior, you can reach the second stage of the Confucian spiritual path. This is called (2) **stopping**, **halting** or **cessation.** This refers to the fact that by watching your thoughts without getting entangled in them, which happens when you practice meditation or mindfulness correctly, your wandering thoughts will slowly die down in volume. You will substantially reduce how often you tend to hold onto thoughts as well as the volume of wandering, random, troublesome, or negative thoughts within your mind. As they leave, eventually your daily mental realm will reach a degree of calmness or purity that we call emptiness, silence, peace, tranquility or mental cessation. This is quieting, halting, stopping or cessation.

This greater mental purity, peace or serenity occurs due to the cessation or stopping (reduction) of random thoughts that naturally occurs by just watching them without attachment. They decline when you do so. Since the mind no longer clings to thoughts with entanglement they will come and go freely, and in this freedom from stickiness your mind will become like a clear mirror that simply reflects or knows thoughts, or we can say it shines light upon them. There are many different ways to describe the same thing.

Thoughts will always keep arising in your mind even when unwanted because they can never be done with. If there is consciousness there will always be thoughts that naturally arise and we cannot control this for that is how consciousness is supposed to work. However, due to meditation and mindfulness practice the volume of random wandering thoughts will die down and the mind will reach a new set-point of background quiet, or cessation, that was not previously existent in your mental realm. In some schools this mental accomplishment is then called "concentration." For instance, when you were a child absorbed in working on a homework problem you would end up silencing all sorts of other wandering thoughts in your mind through focus, and that mental state was called concentration. We can also call that state "clarity" as well as "cessation" because wandering thoughts disappear when you concentrate.

You can sit in meditation and practice mental witnessing in order to attain cessation, a mental quiet characterized by a decline in the volume of wandering thoughts which thereby produces a state of peaceful clarity. This type of practice is called cessation-observation meditation. When not doing sitting meditation practice, by watching your mind during ordinary activities (the regular world) you are also essentially practicing cessation-observation meditation. If you do this often enough and long enough then your mental realm will reach a permanent state of "higher quiet" than if you had not regularly practiced Confucian introspection. This is akin to the "mind like a mirror" of Zen cultivation in that the mind can reflect all things within it clearly without stickiness (attachment) while operating with flawless clarity. Thus you have the "mirror mind" of Buddhism.

The natural result of being mentally mindful of all the contents of your mind is that you stop holding onto thoughts very tightly. You learn to detach, defuse or distance yourself from your thoughts rather than get entangled in them. You begin to see them just as things in your mind rather than reality. Thoughts and emotions then are no longer a pressure you must follow, and in realizing this you may achieve greater independence, detachment or dispassion from thoughts.

Rather than becoming absorbed in your thoughts you can create distance from them by achieving a mindful independent observational vantage so that your actions are not blindly automatic (and thus sometimes harmful) but become thoughtful. By creating some distance from your thoughts you can choose the most proper reaction to your thoughts and can wisely produce better behavior, which is how to cultivate what Confucius called *consummate conduct*. You can more easily override errant thoughts, urges, instincts, impulses, wrong biases, habit energies and emotions through detachment and thereby choose to act in a higher way. By refusing to invest in improper mental processes this unhooking or separation will allow you to move towards a more valuable direction.

A cardinal rule of spiritual practice is also that your thoughts and Qi (internal energy) are linked, and by letting go of your thoughts you let go of Qi flows in your brain and other Qi flows within your body that will now flow more naturally and smoothly without your attachments. Freed of binding restrictions, the Qi in your brain will be released so that it can more fully penetrate all its tissues rather than remain locked in preferred neural circuits that characterize your habitual way of thinking. Through meditation and mindfulness the full set of Qi channels within your brain (where consciousness operates) will thus slowly open up over time, like a flower bud that slowly unfurls to reveal its beauty.

Because of this mental practice your mind will naturally become more quiet because of opened Qi channels; your Qi will be able to flow more freely through the brain without obstructions. The greater mental quiet that you thus achieve is usually called mental cessation or stopping.

In other words, your mind gradually empties of most wandering thoughts (which are often compared to a monkey wildly leaping from tree to tree) due to the practice of watching your thoughts, and so it eventually quiets due to detachment. This is a process of growth that occurs due to consistent meditation practice for those who bother to stay with it. During such practice you should stay aware of your mental realm and its contents, which is alternatively called observance, witnessing, mindfulness, watching, introspection, awareness, knowing or observation. All spiritual schools describe this differently but it is just the same thing – you watch your thoughts like an independent third person observer.

By finding distance from thoughts through mindful observation, you also can achieve a second meaning of stopping or halting, which is to detach from automatically following thoughts as if they were a command or rule you had to obey and follow. You can ignore any feelings that your thoughts and emotions are a pressure that absolutely must be discharged through execution. Thus you can stop errant impulses and negative emotions from manifesting as actions because you can override or ignore them by remaining in transcendence.

By learning how to detach from thoughts you can improve your ability to view them as just mental experiences in your head. Remember that you expect them to reflect truths in the real world, but in many cases they do not, especially when you have added emotional biases to them. Usually they are just guesses as to what is going on.

Through mindful awareness in observing your thoughts you actually give yourself a choice on how much attention to pay to them, and with that distance you can choose to follow just the beneficial thoughts that will help you. This too is a type of cessation or halting – you stop thinking and acting badly - but it applies to improper thinking and behavior. With practice you can learn how to allow thoughts to come and go on their own without any need to hold onto them or push them away, but act only on those that will help you in a positive fashion.

Most religions of the world instruct adherents to meditate using some form of cessation-observation practice and refer to the mental quieting phenomenon under different names. For instance, Buddhism calls the quieting of thoughts the "stilling of the sixth consciousness" or the "attainment (reaching) of emptiness." Vedanta calls it cultivating "pristine awareness" or "pure consciousness." Some schools call this "rectifying the heart" or "calming the passions" and some call it "banishing the lower nature."

All religions essentially refer to the fact that by watching your mind you can quiet thoughts and learn to detach from errant habit energies that would normally automatically impel you. Thus through mental introspection – by always knowing your mind and being aware of your thoughts – you gradually learn control of your behavior. You gradually improve your conduct, which is how you cultivate virtue. This is why humans can rise above the animals who always just follow their impulses. This is also how we learn to cooperate with others or even become heroes who sacrifice themselves for the greater good, which is something that animals never do.

As stated, by mindfully cultivating mental witnessing a noticeable result is that the activity of wild random thoughts dies down in your mind, which then becomes quiet or peaceful as a result. While Buddhism calls this cultivating emptiness or empty mind or no-thought, Confucianism calls this cessation and Christianity calls this internal peace or centering. There are always thoughts in this mental state of greater internal quiet but since the mind seems emptier (more silent or clear) we call it no-thought or emptiness whereas it is never completely quiet. There is just a reduction in the sound volume of our internal dialogue.

At the third stage of the path we can say that this higher degree of mental quiet becomes natural. It is more consistently there, so you reach the third stage of progress (3) called **calming**. When irritating or excitable thoughts are reduced in your mental stream you reach a state of calming and your Qi tends to settle. When your Qi settles this in turn further helps you quiet your thoughts since your Qi and your consciousness are linked.

Basically, the regular practice of sitting meditation together with the constant practice of mental witnessing outside of formal sitting meditation practice leads to a natural emptying of wandering thoughts. Consistent practice gradually opens up the Qi channels in your brain through which energy flows (that affects thought production) and this enables you to reach a more permanent natural level of background mental quiet that is deeper and more stable, which Confucius called calmness. Your mind settles into a homeostasis of clarity and calm at a higher set-point than before.

Because you can now stay in quiet states for more prolonged periods of time this is called "calm abiding" in Tibetan Buddhism. This is the same mental state that everyone achieves except a different name is used to describe the same result. In no case is the mental calming effect you achieve to be considered higher than what is achieved elsewhere via a different spiritual path. Always remember that the results of spiritual practice are non-denominational, accomplished everywhere by everyone who cultivates correctly. Everyone who practices correctly achieves the very same gong-fu. How quickly you attain those results, however, is solely a function of the consistent time spent at proper practice.

When the mind empties itself of most wandering random thoughts and yet remains fully awake and aware (rather than sleepy) it is often called "focus," "one-pointedness" or "concentration" because in being able to maintain calm abiding you are undistracted, and a stable undistracted mind is in a state of a concentration. When the mind becomes calm and stable you can indeed attain the focus of one-pointed concentration. Achieving a continuous state of calm abiding is thus the third step of the cultivation path described by Confucius. This is the third step of cultivating your mind.

Calm abiding doesn't mean you have no thoughts, but that you become more detached from the events of the mind that occur within it and more closely aligned with the quiet observer of your thoughts and emotions who is detached from them. You should be aware of everything that arises within your mind, but also less easily agitated because you are more detached. Your internal dialogue has accordingly died down (along with wandering thoughts) for you to reach this inner calmness, and of what remains you can view it with an unbiased perspective without getting flustered.

Thus, first you practice awareness by watching your mental realm of thoughts. As a result you will gradually achieve a diminishing (cessation) of the wild, random "light" (superficial) wandering thoughts that typically plague the mind. You will achieve a small degree of inner peace or halting of superficial thoughts. By aligning yourself as the observer of thoughts and emotions, through this detachment you can eventually achieve a more profound degree of internal mental peace, stillness, quiet, emptiness, purity, serenity or tranquility that is even more stable.

These then are the first three phases of cultivating mental purity:

awareness, reduction or stopping, and then calming.

Alignment with always being the observer, watcher or witnesser of your thoughts rather than becoming caught up with them leads to freedom from stress, hence calming. This is because the observer function with which you align yourself knows the contents of your mind fully but doesn't identify with them. The observer functions achieves a distance of independence so that you don't lose yourself in worry or become so totally agitated that you end up doing something erratic because you temporarily lost your mind (proper perspective).

This is what we are after as one of the results of spiritual practice. As exemplified by the model of the crystal clear Zen master who always rests joyful in serene composure, it is one of the non-denominational results of the spiritual path.

If your mind can become calm because you detach from thoughts through witnessing practice and you remain in that state for a long time, Confucius said that your continuous cultivation of calmness can lead to (4) an even more purified mental realm called "**stillness**." You can also think of this as equanimity where there don't seem to be any thoughts. Aligning with the silent witness or observer that is *you* brings quiet, peace, purity, non-judgment and hence equanimity. Thoughts die down even more to a state of quiet called no-thought.

Buddhism and Hinduism explain that at this stage of mental progress you have transcended the ordinary level of coarse thoughts that typically plague the mental realm of a human being. You have touched upon no-thought, and are now on the cultivation path of the saints and sages.

You are less inclined to be engaged in coarse thinking at this stage because you have somewhat purified what we might call the ordinary human level of gross mentality. You understand your thoughts are entities/objects within your mind that can be manipulated rather than commands that must be followed. This is how you elevate yourself to a higher level of being and spiritualize your life. This is how you transcend the functions of your mind. It all starts with purifying your mind through awareness by cutting off errant thoughts while selecting better thoughts instead, and never getting caught up in them.

Hinduism explains that through meditation you become free of both the *vitarka* and *vicara* types of thoughts, which are coarse and more subtle types of mental grasping, and thus your mind becomes extremely empty or still, which is the pristine clarity mentioned in Vedanta or Zen. Actually, this mental result is just a mundane thing – your mind seems a little more empty and clear, that's all, but of course this is a prize we all want to win because of the peace and other benefits it provides. While technical terms say that you "transcend coarse conceptuality and analysis" this just means that your mind is now pretty clear and your thoughts are not as wild and haphazard as before you started to practice. Once again, this is how you slowly elevate your mentality above the normal runnings of an animal, which is the entire purpose of spiritual practice.

After this clarity-stillness-concentration attainment, Confucius explained that the next (fifth) stage of achievement is that you (5) can attain **bliss.** Physical bliss, which is due to the opening and enervation of Qi channels all throughout your body since your Qi can now run through what has been opened with an improved flow rate, is not attained in a short while, but only after years of cultivation practice from teaching the mind how to settle. As Mencius explained, he had to consistently cultivate his Qi to attain his stage of achievement.

Many cultivation schools, such as Yoga and Vajrayana, use special practices to cultivate the body's Qi and channels. Mental witnessing practitioners of all schools, including Zen, Vedanta, and Confucianism, should use these internal energy practices as well rather than just engage in quieting meditation practice alone. For instance, pranayama breathing practices greatly help in this regard.

As one Japanese Zen master once said, you not only must cultivate your mind and purify it to bring out its brightness, but you have to match this effort of mindfulness with internal energy practices to transform your body. The spiritual path is a *mind-body* pathway of cultivation, and the necessity of dual practice is something you must never forget.

In Confucianism, bliss represents the *combined result* of physical bliss due to excellent Qi cultivation, mental quiet (emptiness or no-thought), and clear awareness. You feel happy because your mind is less filled with distractions and is more clear and peaceful. This fifth step of attainment basically means you achieve an even higher stage of calm, empty mental concentration that is accompanied now by physical bliss too. The benefit of your meditation practice has opened up your Qi channels over time and now your body's Qi flows more smoothly within you, producing a subtle feeling of physical comfort. With the body now comfortable, one is better able to ignore it to attain yet a greater degree of mental clarity and concentration.

As with Confucianism, Buddhism also explains that consistent meditation practice will help you reach a state of bliss and one-pointed concentration while the Hindu Yoga schools also speak of your being able to attain a blissful feeling samadhi (concentration) through consistent spiritual practice. Bliss is like a clear, empty mind conjoined with an internal glow of physical feeling that results from excellent Qi flow, which is why athletes sometimes attain it, and also entails a happiness resulting from a quiet, serene mind free of agitations.

After attaining bliss as a foundational basis, Confucius said that you will then reach the sixth stage of progress. With the body peaceful and calm experiencing pleasant feelings that don't bother you, and with your mind open and at ease experiencing clarity, your natural wisdom will be able to open up and you can become able (6) to attain "**right knowing**" or "correct thinking." You will become able to think correctly without incorrect bias or prejudice. You will see those bias and correct them.

This is the sixth stage of the path. It means you are not overly biased, prejudiced or emotional your and thus can arrive at the best conclusions with your thought processes. If you can keep from melding with selfish thoughts, biases and emotions that might arise to cloud the mirror of your mind, your mental processes free of such pollutions will more accurately reflect the true dimensions and features of every situation that comes before them, thus enabling you to arrive at better thinking. Thinking that is unencumbered by irrelevancies, irrationalities or emotions and biases can silence prejudicial likes and dislikes to approach the highest stages of rationality or wisdom, i.e. wise thinking.

This is right thinking or correct thought, which is the apex of spirituality. Right thinking does not necessarily mean that your thinking conclusions are always correct, for you can always make errors in thinking. Instead it means that you arrived at a conclusion using the clearest thought processes and highest decision models available to you. Right knowing/thinking is a process of filtering or weeding out erroneous mental influences, especially biases and emotions that are "mere opinion" and thus termed "selfish" in Confucianism. Confucian self-cultivation is a process of filtering out such erroneous influences in all you think, say and do.

The pathway to right knowing or right thinking entails mindfulness of thoughts because mindfulness, in viewing thoughts as an observer, unhooks us from thoughts back to direct experience so that we can look at thoughts as objects in the mind rather than absolute truths or commands we must follow. Being detached from thoughts you can choose which ones to act upon and which ones to ignore. This gives you the maximum amount of power to manipulate them.

Separating yourself from a fusion with your thoughts, desirous impulses and emotions, you can rise above the contents of your mind and actualize righting thinking. Like Sherlock Holmes you can arrive at more useful insights and better conclusions because you employ logic and clarity rather than emotions and prejudices.

This is the equivalent of proper thinking, correct reasoning, wise discrimination, discriminative analysis, good judgment, wisdom or understanding in Buddhism. You can think correctly clear of prejudices and make good judgments without bias. Wisdom is not just what you think or how you think but how you relate to the thoughts which arise within you. Thoughts are not something happening to you in the real world but in the mental sphere, so you must recognize that they aren't necessarily true, and that you can detach from them and ignore them.

It is through wisdom, or proper discrimination, that you can finally realize the true nature of your mind. This is the fact that when there are thoughts or objects in your consciousness then this is objective knowledge, but when there are no objects or thoughts in the mind then the mind is experienced as quiet, empty or peaceful. This second option is called pure consciousness or emptiness or pure awareness; the mind is quiet but not absolutely inert because it is ready to know the thoughts that will arise. This is your bright virtue.

This finding or realization about the nature of the mind constitutes (7) **attainment**, which is the seventh stage of the Confucian path. It is sometimes called the realization of bright virtue (or emptiness in Buddhism) since awareness or consciousness is your miraculous capability.

The miracle of the universe is the evolution of life with consciousness, namely awareness and knowingness. As a living being you have a mind with thoughts you can control or manipulate, and that mind is your field of bright virtue that has (a) clear awareness, brightness or pristine consciousness with the ability to know (b) and the ability to generate thoughts, namely the ability to create mental objects to know.

This is sentience, cognizance, awareness, illumination or consciousness. You are blessed with the ability to know and understand whereas insentient things, which vastly outnumber you in the universe, lack this miraculous ability. Your mind is therefore the wish-fulfilling gem of Buddhism that can help you attain anything you want. Of course you don't get what you wish for but only what you work for, but your mind is what allows you to understand this and accomplish the getting or creation of a future you want. Consciousness – your mind - is your wish-fulfilling gem.

While some spiritual schools such as Buddhism or Vedanta focus on the I-thought or I-center as being crucial for the ability to know, and while sometimes they focus on explaining the detailed processes of sense perception turning into consciousness, in Confucianism it is enough for people to simply recognize that the ability of consciousness itself is the great gift, miracle, merit or virtue of human beings. This is our bright virtue, which is the power of cognizant illumination.

Thoughts automatically arise in your mind seemingly from nothingness when they appear due to stimuli, but you can also generate them yourself for whatever reasons you desire, including the desire to express the highest models of virtue that you know. Your mind is actually a wish-fulfilling gem that allows you to have awareness/consciousness and generate the thoughts you need to accomplish or experience whatever you want. Your mind is your source of light, your source of awareness/consciousness, your source of cognizance or illumination. Your mind of clear/bright awareness is your merit, your field of bright virtue.

All your prior mindfulness and meditation practice has laid the foundation for this achievement of spiritual success where you can *see your mind clearly and know all of the comings and goings inside it with clarity*. This is a spiritual result, but this is an ordinary mundane result too since this is just the ordinary mind. The result of Confucian cultivation is the perfection of consciousness achieved by cultivating mental clarity, or self-knowledge, and correct thinking. This is the key to higher spiritual accomplishments that elevate us from being just ordinary animals.

At this last stage of attainment you are now not so confused or controlled by the contents of your mind, and so now it can be fully used as a magical tool of creation, a wish-fulfilling gem, an instrument of bright virtue. Your mind can be quiet/pure, and your thoughts can also become pure by becoming populated by virtuous ideas to compassionately help people rather than harm others. That is the definition of spirituality; it is all about how you use your mind in terms of thoughts and their expression as behavior.

To get to the stage of attainment you quieted your mind through meditation and self-observation, cultivated distraction-free concentration and mindful watching to quiet it even further, and then within the resulting clarity realized the nature of your mind where it has no thoughts but always gives birth to thoughts that pass away. It is always generating thoughts naturally in response to inputs by the senses and prior thoughts, and you can also use it to intentionally create thoughts by will. How you use it is what makes you a saint or a devil, an animal or man who models himself on the ideal of the highest possible person.

There are thousands of functions that your consciousness can perform. It can function in all sorts of ways learning countless skills. You can certainly learn to manipulate your thoughts this way or that way because you learn all sorts of mental skills but *your thoughts are never you*. They are mental objects that appear in your consciousness, or bright virtue, which is an open visage of what seems like silence, space or emptiness that you can compare to the peacefulness, quiet, emptiness or stillness of the original nature.

Of the thousands of thoughts always flitting through your mind, you have the ability to choose the highest virtuous ones, which you should display through the most proper words and behavior. This is the desired end result of spiritual cultivation and the seventh stage of the Confucian path. With the mind now available as a flexible tool capable of correct thinking processes free of emotional baggage, you can choose to use it rightly to help humanity. This is correct thinking, which is using the mind not just to help yourself but to help others for by lifting everyone else up you lift yourself up as well.

These are the seven steps in the Confucian pathway to cultivating your mind and ultimately becoming a sage.

CHAPTER 5:
THE CONFUCIAN RANKS
OF SPIRITUAL ATTAINMENT

The Confucian Shao Yang said, "We know that man is the highest among the objects, and that a sage is the highest among men. The highest of men is he who can observe 10,000 minds by one mind; who can observe 10,000 bodies with one body; who lives in one generation yet can understand 10,000 generations."

This is no different than the enlightenment teachings of many other religions concerning the capabilities of a sage. For instance, Buddhism states that an enlightened Buddha (equivalent to a Confucian sage) can know people's minds by emanating out, from his Supra-Causal enlightenment body composed of Later Heavenly Qi, *nirmanakaya* projection bodies composed of lesser substances that can enter into people. Thus possessing their bodies and minds and being able to see things through their memories, this is how a sage can know your thoughts as well as give you new helpful thoughts from his own mind. This is how a sage helps people, which is by projecting versions of himself (composed of higher energetic substances) into them with the objective of giving them both thoughts and energy. When you call on a Buddha for help, this is primarily what they try to do to assist you - they project versions of themselves into you or others in order to give thoughts to help.

Chinese culture commonly speaks of the ascending essences or matter states of Jing, Qi, Shen, Later Heavenly Qi (energy) and Primordial Heavenly Qi (energy). These are the states that compose the higher body attainments of a sage that together form the Reward Body or Enjoyment Body of enlightenment called the *sambhogakaya* in Buddhism. The Reward body of a sage is actually a chain of duplicate bodies composed of different substances linked together – a physical body made of flesh, subtle body composed of Qi, Causal body composed of Shen, Supra-Causal body composed of Later Heavenly energy, and Immanence body composed of Primordial Heavenly energy. When humans die we are said to be ejected from the human frame with bodies of Qi, which is why we becomes spirits or devas, but the spiritual bodies of sages are more complicated because they cultivated these higher bodies of more elevated substances when alive, and they come attendant with incredible capabilities.

Most every cultivation school has various ranks to mark out milestones on the path of spiritual attainment. These naturally correspond to mental, behavioral and body achievements. For instance, Buddhism has four levels of progressive spiritual attainment that delineate an Arhat, or enlightened one. There are the *Sotapanna, Sakadagami, Anagami* and *Arhat* stages of enlightenment attainment followed by the fifth level of a fully enlightened Buddha, who possesses the Immanence body aforementioned. A fully enlightened Buddha cultivates a large "Reward body" composed of the human body made of flesh (Jing), deva body made of Qi, Causal body composed of Shen, Supra-Causal body composed of Later Heavenly Qi and Immanence body composed of Primordial Heavenly Qi (energy) all linked together. All of these bodies attached together, with each one composed of a higher or lower level of essence, comprise the *sambhogakaya* or Reward body of enlightenment. A spiritual master uses these different bodies to do various things in the universe, helping people wherever they can in whatever ways they can, but mostly by giving them thoughts and energy (such as for healing purposes) when appropriate.

Some of the higher bodies, such as the Supra-Causal, can project off many tethered versions of themselves made of lower energies. Then they can use these *nirmanakaya* or emanation bodies to possess people when necessary in order to help a situation by giving them thoughts or energy. A spiritual master trains to be able to use all of his lower bodies independently so that it seems as if he is present in each realm where a lower body resides, but he/she is usually off elsewhere because he/she will always primarily reside in the realm of his/her highest body. The idea that a master is in an unmovable samadhi trance is therefore just nonsense because it usually means that his spirit bodies are out elsewhere occupied doing something. This is why he/she often seems to have vacant eyes or is non-responsive.

Starting from the level of a human being, Chinese Taoism also has various stages of Immortals that also correspond to these same Buddhist Arhat stages of attainment. These are the Earthly, Spiritual, and Celestial ranks of Immortals.

Representing Hinduism, the Hindu sage Sri Siddharameshwar Maharaj also taught that we have the Physical, Subtle, Causal, Supra-Causal and Para-atman bodies that exactly correspond to same five essence bodies previously mentioned. Each new body attainment corresponds to a higher rank of spiritual achievement, and those ranks exactly match with the ranks taught within Buddhism and Taoism.

Ramalinga, representing the Tamil Siddha and Nath Yoga traditions, taught that the stages of cultivation achievement start with the coarse Physical body and then through Qi cultivation, as mentioned by Mencius, one can attain a purified Qi body, body of Vibrations (made of Shen), Wisdom Light body (made of Later Heavenly energy) and then Body of Immanence. In Ramalinga's tradition these five bodies are the *Stuhla deha, Suddha deha, Mantra deha, Jnana deha* (*Divya deha* or body of light, *Kailaya deha*), and Body of Immanence. They are also the same five body attainments.

Vajrayana (Tantric Buddhism) also talks about the Physical body, Impure illusory body (subtle or deva body), Purified illusory body, Wisdom light (Clear Light) or Dharma body, and then the Buddha body composed of very subtle fundamental wind (energies). Together these comprise the exact same *sambhogakaya* Reward body and stages of attainment.

In Confucianism we also have five bodies, and we call an enlightened individual a sage. In any spiritual school, including Confucianism, to reach the status of a fully enlightened sage you must progress through prior stages of spiritual attainment that involve using your internal energy to cultivate higher spiritual bodies as just described. Only step-by-step progress allows you to reach the fully enlightened attainment of a sage.

During this progression, with each new spiritual body attainment your mind becomes more clear and bright, which is why mental clarity is emphasized on the Confucian path and in other cultivation traditions. Cultivation schools typically focus on describing the ultra clear mind-stream corresponding to an Arhat's body attainment. Nearly every spiritual sect will not talk about body attainments, however, because practitioners referencing this yardstick will easily become disheartened knowing they have not achieved the fruit. However, by describing the spiritual path in terms of mental clarity and emptiness (which offers an analogy to the emptiness of the original nature), practitioners will continue cultivating with hope since they aren't clear about their true stage of progress. This is why most schools describe the path in terms of consciousness rather than bodies, which is so that cultivators always keep practicing.

Someone who is enlightened has attained a spiritual body whose mind-stream and body, due to being composed of more subtle energies than the coarse physical nature, is often compared to light because of the analogy with awareness and illumination, but they are not any wiser nor think any better than we do since that body is simply a duplicate of their human body, its habit energies and its regular thought patterns. Nevertheless, this achievement is the spiritual path, which is a progressive attainment of higher and higher spiritual bodies that are limited to five in teachings although how far one can reach is much higher.

You have seen the names for these bodies/stages used by other traditions, but few know that Confucianism has them as well. Mencius provided us a list of these stages of spiritual attainment that is similar to the ranks found in other religions, once again attesting to the non-denominational nature of the spiritual path. The way that you achieve these attainments is the same as elsewhere, namely that you must cultivate both your mind and body along with your behavior. To attain these higher bodies also requires the devoted assistance of sages gone before you who must you lend you their energy to help transform your body, and none will be committed to helping you for such a long process if you are not a virtuous human being working on perfecting your behavior.

Goodness or Kindness

In terms of stages, Mencius said that the foundation of the spiritual path starts with the desire to cultivate. He called this beginner's stage **"goodness"** or **"kindness"** because the spiritual path is founded upon a basis of refraining from evil ways while pursuing virtue and morality instead. This is cultivating kindness, goodness, virtue or compassion as a human being. Thus the first stage of kindness or goodness.

In every religious tradition you must cultivate virtue, morality, benevolence, compassion, kindness or goodness as the foundation of the spiritual path, so it's no revelation to find this same emphasis by Chinese sages. Once entering the gate of the spiritual road you are immediately set on the pathway of doing good deeds while eschewing evil thoughts and behavior, so Mencius called "goodness" the first stage of cultivation. This is the cultivation stage of a human being with a coarse material body.

All throughout their lives, and especially after they succeed, people must practice virtuous ways and work to elevate their minds as basic spiritual practice, which is the practice of self-perfection. This is the core of the spiritual path as well as its end result so it involves cultivating, perfecting or purifying your mind, words and behavior.

This is why the Confucian way involves learning meditation and mindfulness. Meditation helps you form the habit of watching your mind and behavior so that you can correct your personal faults and flaws, and mindfulness helps you do this in real time. This method of training helps you to become a virtuous person, namely a top level human being.

Faith or Belief

The next stage of spiritual progress in Confucianism is called "**faith**" or "**belief**" because belief arises when an individual starts to attain some substantial results from their cultivation efforts. Then they believe in it. An individual who works hard attains the initial fruit of the path, which is the deva body or subtle body attainment made of Qi that is called the first dhyana attainment in Buddhism. Because of attaining the deva body whilst alive, a practitioner starts believing in the entirety of the pathway teachings. Upon gaining access to the heavenly deva realm an aspirant will spend time going back and forth from his physical body to this subtle realm. He will converse with all the devas and discover the truth about the rest of the spiritual path, so of course he will then gain faith in the teachings.

In Buddhism the stage of Faith is attained when someone reaches the first dhyana, which is the *Sotapanna* Arhat stage and the very first rank of higher spiritual body achievements. An individual at this true belief stage of Buddhism has attained the independent subtle body or deva body that can leave the physical body shell at will. This is the astral body of western mysticism, impure illusory body of Vajrayana, *suddha deha* of the Tamil siddhas, or *yin shen* body of Taoism. It is an exact duplicate of your physical body, composed of Qi and free of disease, that can leave the body at will to enter the lowest spiritual realms of the earth that people go to upon death but which they call "heaven."

With this body one can converse with other spiritual beings. Thus with access to untainted spiritual teachings and the ability to know the truth, no one can cheat the new initiate about the spiritual path. They can no longer be confused by many false religious teachings in the world and so they develop trust and faith in the path. Since they establish trust, confidence, faith and belief in the path of cultivation (from having attained the first fruit of an independent spirit body), Mencius called this the stage of Belief or Faith.

Beauty

The next stage of spiritual progress in Confucianism is called "**beauty**." In order to keep progressing you must cultivate the Qi of this new subtle body to a higher stage of purity just as devas must do. Buddhism and Hinduism state that this is what heavenly devas occupy themselves with perfecting to reach a yet higher body attainment, which is composed of Shen. Since an ordinary deva and human Faith stage attainee now have the same type of deva body composed of Qi, this need for further purification necessitates that the deva level of attainment is differentiated into two classification levels. In Buddhism your initial development of the subtle body corresponds to the first dhyana while a higher degree of its Qi purification (corresponding to the devas' efforts at purification) is termed the second dhyana attainment.

Mencius called the efforts of this stage "extending and fulfilling," meaning that by further Qi and channel purification of your Qi body you can reach a higher stage of its purification, but it is not yet a new body composed of Shen. In other words, you can cultivate your subtle body attainment, composed of Qi, to reach a more purified level of the Qi-based complex of subtle body and mind but it isn't an *extra body*.

This attainment is called Beauty and is equivalent to the second dhyana of Buddhism. You first attain the deva body and then you continue cultivating it, "extending and fulfilling it," which is called beautifying it or perfecting it. You must do this before you can generate an additional Shen body out of its essence just as you generated a Qi body out of the essence of your physical body. Normally people simply eject a coarse level deva body out of their physical body upon death, but the one a sage generates is far more purified and has higher capabilities.

Greatness or Grandness

Mencius said that from the stage of Beauty as a base, "extending and fulfilling it until it shines forth is called great." "Greatness" or "grandness" is the name for the next spiritual body attainment composed of Shen. It corresponds to the third dhyana attainment of Buddhism, which is also called the Causal body in Hinduism and Shen body attainment in Taoism. It is a body tethered to the Qi body but composed of a more refined substance than Qi.

Remember that spiritual schools never explain spiritual attainments in terms of bodies but in terms of consciousness achievements so that people don't become disheartened at their lack of spiritual progress. They want people to always be cultivating virtue and clarity of mind to raise themselves above animal behavior, so they speak of spiritual attainments in terms of a pure mind and pure (virtuous) behavior. On purpose they exclude the fact that the spiritual path is all about attaining higher and higher bodies. They speak of consciousness or pure mind achievements instead, leading people onwards with phrases such as "cultivate emptiness" and "realize the root source of the mind" which motivate people to meditate and master mental watching. They do this, focusing on "purifying consciousness," so that practitioners always keep cultivating while never losing hope that they will one day "become enlightened."

The truth is that no spiritual beings will make a commitment to spend substantial time to help you attain the higher spiritual bodies unless you are virtuous, ethical and moral. Therefore religions are designed to cultivate virtue, morality and cooperation in populations, with few people altruistic enough to be able to attain the higher bodies.

This not communicating the whole truth is an example of the "skillful means" (i.e. *Lotus Sutra* method) used across the world by enlightened individuals when they teach and why Mencius therefore described the Greatness spiritual stage as the mind "shining forth with its fullness" that transcends the subtle realm of earth-bound devas. This corresponds to a Causal, Shen-based or *Mantra deha* body.

According to Vajrayana Buddhism, on the spiritual path your impure illusory body (subtle or deva body) can generate from within it a purified illusory body, free from all gross matter and impurities, at this stage of attainment that Mencius called Grandness. The Nath Yoga tradition calls it a "body of vibrations" to refer to its composition of a higher form of energy (Shen) than Qi. It is composed of an even more refined (higher) form of energy or substance. Mencius said that to reach the stage of Greatness and then transform it is to reach the stage of the sage, which is the next stage of achievement.

The Sage

When the sensory reach of your mind becomes exceedingly large (called "infinite without boundaries" although this is an exaggeration) because you attain a Supra-Causal body, which is the next attainment level, this is the enlightenment of an Arhat or Buddha. With this body, composed of Later Heavenly Qi, your mind-body vehicle is composed of a substance that transcends all lower energies, including Qi and Shen, which is why it can sense vibrations or perturbations within all the denser realms.

This is the capability of a Buddha, or we can say the "enlightenment" of a Buddha. Mencius calls this stage of cultivation a "**sage**." It corresponds to the Buddhist/Hindu enlightenment stage of realizing the clear light, uncreated light, or clear aspect of the mind called pure consciousness. Actually, what this really means is that your newest Supra-Causal body – which is still attached to your previous Causal, subtle and human bodies – is composed of a substance, essence or energy so pure that our only comparison of its purity is to light.

Consciousness at this stage, as with all stages, is still dependent upon the structure and functioning of your body vehicle since it is still an exact replica of your physical body. Are you any wiser than a human at this stage of attainment? You might be able to know more, but you still have the same thinking processes and habits that you did prior to this attainment unless you study more, work hard, undergo many experiences and keep perfecting yourself and your abilities with these new bodies. Every new body is simply a replica of your previous lower body with all of these bodies dependent upon your original human body as the template, and thus your thinking processes stay the same with each new body. The only thing that is different are the new skills you gain with the new body, whose capabilities you must learn to master.

Naturally each new body will have more capabilities and can accumulate more experiences than the lower body it was generated from, but the memories of the new body are not imprinted in the lower ones. Furthermore, when a master is operating in the world while his higher body is busy elsewhere in higher realms he will often seem as if not present, and only when the higher bodies return to rest in his lowest physical shell will he seem to make wiser decisions than when he/she seems absent.

Divineness (*Shen*)

In progressing upwards, when an enlightened person's cultivation level becomes so high that nobody knows how high it is, Confucianism calls this the stage of being a "*shen*" (divine), which is equivalent to the highest level of the Buddhist enlightenment *bhumis*. This stage of divineness is akin to a fully enlightened Buddha of perfect and complete enlightenment. This is the body of the Immanence attainment composed of Primordial Heavenly Qi/energy.

This is sometimes called the stage of "no mind and no body" where it is said that one has become "oned" with the *Taiji*, or Supreme Ultimate. At this stage it is said that you become unknowable or unfathomable and thus unpredictable, able to liberate beings all over the universe. Of course, this is only a type of expedient teaching since there are higher body attainments available still.

In terms of the path itself to enlightenment (becoming a sage), Confucius did not describe the spiritual pathway as Mencius did, but simply described the general cultivation path in terms of how you should practice cultivating your mind and behavior, without which you cannot attain these higher attainments, and what one should expect along the way.

In *The Great Learning*, Confucius explained that the whole purpose and highest potential of human life was to engage in this "Great Learning," whose highest stage of attainment makes us a cosmic being able to help countless other beings in the universe. This is what Confucianism and the other religions are really all about, but few people ever learn about these esoteric details.

CHAPTER 6:
CULTIVATING VIRTUE TO BRIGHTEN
ONE'S CHARACTER AND FORTUNE

Confucian cultivation emphasizes the practice of mindfulness, which means watching your mind to know your thoughts clearly. You practice mental watching so that you can cultivate a realm of mental purity.

Mental purity means two things: (a) achieving a higher degree of inner mental quiet and clarity where you know your thoughts clearly (you know what you are thinking rather than remain oblivious of the fact), and (b) generating "higher thoughts" or "virtuous thoughts" that are more pure because they rise above your baser instincts and urges. These two aspects of mental purity are the basis of human ennoblement and higher spiritual attainments.

Mastering our mental sphere and our behavior is what separates us from animals whose consciousness focuses on eating to satisfy hunger, drinking to satisfy thirst, copulating to satisfy carnal urges, and remaining on constant fearful alert in order to avoid being eaten. Confucian cultivation of our mind helps us avoid becoming bestial due to unchecked passions, wishes and desires. It helps us transcend our lower nature and become the higher possible person. What is this process of ennoblement? It is using our rational mind of clarity to transcend and purify the irrational parts of our consciousness that are the vestiges of our animal nature.

Mental purity and clarity – because they allow you to police your thoughts, words and behavior – are exactly the very things that also enable you to change your fortune to become better and eventually enter the realm

44

of the sages. Of course achieving the level of a "sage" or "worthy" requires considerable individual effort past a rudimentary mastery of mindfulness. Nevertheless, every sage starts upon the spiritual path of ennoblement and transcendence by watching their thoughts so that they always know their mind clearly, and through this activity the background noise in their mind eventually dies down over time.

Knowing his thoughts and watching his behavior, a sage immediately cuts off faults and errors whenever he notices them so as to always be pursuing virtue and always be improving situations for the better. Those who strive to become sages are those who wish to take human culture to the highest levels of ennoblement. They work on becoming morally better people, more careful in handing affairs, and more active in benefitting the world around them so that people can attain a life of human flourishing.

You too are inherently a sage. You possess the inherent capability of a sage, as do all human beings, and can bring out this potential through Confucian training. The practices of meditation and mindfulness in daily life to produce proper behavior are the tools that make this happen. When your thoughts turn away from the low towards ennoblement, such as taking a vow to improve the welfare of others, you have entered upon the path of the sages. By cultivating altruistic virtuous behavior you make your life meaningful. By no longer focusing solely on your self and your desires, you become part of the great reset movement that is trying to renew the world.

The ennoblement of human beings as a group will only happen when we all devote ourselves to higher thoughts and behavior that cultivate our cooperative humanity to help society move forward. Intimately bound with others, when we work to alleviate the sufferings of a group we also eliminate our own burdens. And when everyone pursues altruistic actions to help the greater whole they will build a culture that is maximally rewarding in every direction.

Like Christianity, the Confucian way especially emphasizes the practice of virtuous behavior for becoming a better human being. It also emphasizes contributing to humanity or larger social groups in a way that will create prosperity and harmoniousness. This type of activity feeds our higher nature.

No animal in nature tries to improve itself or cooperatively sacrifices itself for a group of others. However, the human drive for self-perfection and altruistic action is the natural outcome of cultivating mental watching, mental purity and a life of activity in tune with virtue and propriety. No animal chooses to consciously change itself; only humans consciously choose to improve themselves in a way they desire. Among other things, what distinguishes us from animals is the ability to set upon a path of self-improvement where an individual takes control of his life through cultivation practice and tries to make of himself whatever he wills. An individual lives his life in harmony with higher values he selects in order to make something special of his life. You can become the possible person, the ideal you have of your individual purpose.

Just as is transmitted in the Ten Commandments of Christianity or emphasized in the *Yamas* and *Niyamas* of Hindu Yoga, the task of cultivating virtuous behavior is to be regarded as the core foundation of human life because it creates higher human culture. Virtuous behavior, including discipline of various types, is what elevates us above the vicious kill-or-be-killed realm of animals where the powerful oppress the weak without restraint. This is why ethical conduct is the foundational bedrock for all the paths of religion.

Animals need strength and cunning to survive, but man can rise above the realm of vicious creatures and their cruel tendency to kill one another. He can make a conscious decision to rise above his animal nature despite his biological instincts. For instance, this is why many religions espouse temporary periods of fasting and celibacy, which teach men that they can rise above their biological desires such as hunger and sexual gratification. Men can be taught to rise above their lusts and passions – their animal heritage – and become free of their lower nature. The goal of such practices is to teach us that we can cultivate patience, self-discipline, forbearance and transcendence. We can rise above our impulses even though they be strong, and that we are more than the sum of our biological urges.

Man can transcend the natural tendency to selfishly satisfy desires by cultivating self-discipline and virtue, which define what it means to be human. Aristotle felt that happiness was a life of activity lived in accordance with virtue, and this was a life lived meaningfully. Socrates taught the same principle, and so did Jesus. Confucius also taught that a man must follow the virtuous path at the cost of life itself. Why do all religions share this commonality?

Through his powers of consciousness and by virtue of positive character traits, man can create civilization and culture. With culture life is no longer about survival alone but about meaning. With culture one can find purposes within life. In the quest for meaning man creates society based upon the principles of virtue. Culture is what enables us to rise above bestiality, and culture is based upon communication, cooperation (where you don't take your own desires as preeminent), discipline and virtue.

The Confucian way is the road of generating higher culture. The method is to harmonize cooperative relationships between people and have individuals start watching their thoughts, speech and behavior to rise above motivations of greed, power, and selfishness. It involves teaching people to take themselves out of egotism in order to benefit others. It is utopian nonsense to believe that all people will do this or become this way. However, the Confucian ideal is that teaching this path widely will lead to many following its pathway of self-perfection.

The pathway of pursuing virtue is not an inner mental game that never projects itself into the outer world. It involves interactions with others - greater society - via actual deeds and relationships. It is a special emphasis of Confucius that we try to act compassionately and harmonize our cooperative interactions with other people. It is also a special emphasis that as soon as you recognize that you are involved in errant behavior, especially activity that might harm others, you should immediately stop doing it.

Mencius explained, "Suppose there is a person who every day appropriates one of his neighbor's chickens. Someone tells him, 'This is not the Way of an exemplary individual.' He then says, 'May I reduce it to appropriating one chicken every month and wait until next year to stop?' If one knows that it is not righteous, then one should quickly stop."

Putting it frankly, whenever you know that your behavior is wrong then you must stop at that point. You stop when you recognize that you are in the wrong. Isn't this what we normally demand of others? Isn't this what we try to teach our children?

Confucius and Mencius both emphasized that human beings be straightforward, honest and sincere. They insisted that people show consideration for others and practice benevolence (consummate conduct) by engaging in ethical, moral, virtuous, proper, righteous behavior. This is the pathway to becoming a true human being because you are following your greater self rather than lesser self. You are putting aside your animalistic tendencies and rising above them through ennoblement.

The Great Learning required of life is the challenge to rise above the attitudes, thoughts and instincts that might impel you to choose a lower pathway of behavior in each and every situation you encounter, and choosing the highest effective pathway instead. This is spiritualizing your behavior. This is the pathway of the sage.

The basic form of Confucian self-correction is called cessation-observation practice or mindfulness, which entails watching your mind. This is the most basic of spiritual practices commonly found across the world's religions. At the very minimum it will help you to become a better human being. At a higher level of expertise it will help you change your fortune, and with even more skillfulness this behavior will improve your health and even your longevity. At its apex of mastery it will lead you to becoming a sage and teacher of mankind. Simply observe your mind, discover what thoughts lead you to a fuller, better, higher or more meaningful life, and follow those ideas rather than weld yourself to a lower state of beingness and behavior.

Both Confucius and Socrates said that even if you face poverty or death you must always choose the pathway of spiritual ennoblement. You must do what is right even at the cost of your life. For instance, when ordered to arrest a man named Leon from Salamis so that he could be unjustly executed, Socrates returned to his home refusing to do so even though he knew it probably meant his own death. Socrates knew what he was told to do was wrong and so he refused to follow those instructions.

The basic methodology of spiritualization, self-improvement or self-correction to be practiced by everyone - including the highest emperor and most humble commoner - entails always observing, witnessing, observing or knowing your thoughts like a third person observer who sees them as objects appearing in the mind that might have to be corrected. You must train to be an observer of your thoughts and actions and clearly know what is happening inside and outside your mind. When you see your thoughts or behavior moving in the wrong direction, when you know something is wrong, then when this comes to your attention you must pull yourself back onto the proper path.

Thoughts are just experiences in your head rather than absolute realities. They are just representations of the world and situations that are sometimes falsities or illusions. In just being ideas they are not commands you need always follow. They are just guesses as to what is going on. They are the objects or products of consciousness, which is our miraculous blessing of cognizance, and being such we need to learn what to do with them. It is which thoughts you choose to follow and how you respond to them that matters most in life.

Rather than worship, "knowing your mind" is the basis of the most effective forms of spiritual practice across the world yet no one tells you this. You are the one who has to become spiritualized, and self-cultivation of your thoughts and behavior is the means to do so. Purifying your mind because of correcting your thoughts is a higher spiritual method than any act of worship.

How are we to practice this correctly so that we get better at it and the results permanently penetrate through to regular life? How are we to engage upon the path of mental purification, which means spiritual purification, so that we are permanently better human beings?

Thoughts operate on their own, arising when you need them according to circumstances, and they depart when no longer needed. They are generated automatically by the mind because this is the nature of consciousness, and the rule of consciousness is that the flow of automatic thoughts cannot be stopped. For instance, when you concentrate on some task at hand you always develop the thoughts you need. They are generated as you need them.

This ability to form the right thoughts is just a natural capability of the mind. When you don't need to concentrate on a topic anymore then those thoughts will naturally leave you and your mind will start wandering in distractedness once again, moving from one thing to another looking for involvement while being jostled by external stimuli. Since thought generation never stops, the question for us then becomes how to deal with them properly, yet no one teaches us any principles about this in our educational systems.

Here is the solution. A man of cultivation trains to become master of his mind. He trains to master all the functions of his mind, including the automatic functions of unwanted thoughts that may plague him. He trains to control his attitude. He learns how to master his powers of focus and concentration, his thought generation and selection process, and how to deal with mental afflictions and distractions that naturally arise. As the great philosopher William James said, "The greatest discovery of my generation is that a human being can alter his life by altering his attitudes." A man learns to do this by developing control over his mind.

Mastering the mind starts with awareness, which is to know the contents of one's mind (one's thoughts). With awareness, by steps one learns concentration and how to ignore or decrease unhelpful thoughts and distractions that automatically arise. One also learns how to give rise to, select or manipulate thoughts as needed.

We can choose to become one of two types of human beings. We can (1) strive to always be in a clear state of knowing concentration wherein we know the thoughts flowing through our minds. Or, (2) we can choose to remain an individual who easily becomes distracted or agitated and thus entangled in thoughts or a loser of mental clarity. If you don't cultivate then wandering thoughts and desires will predominate in your mind, obscure your present purpose and make you their prisoner.

The pathway of the clear mind that knows its contents develops a higher vantage point of dispassionate wisdom while the distracted, undisciplined mind remains mired in a realm of unclearness that easily leads to harm, wrongdoing or animalistic tendencies.

Sloppy mental habits can entangle us in clinging to our thoughts so that we lose an independent perspective, and this loss can lead to wrong decisions. We must learn how to properly discriminate between right and wrong, and further recognize that our thoughts are not absolutes. They do not necessarily embody an accurate take on reality but are just potential guidelines for opinions and behaviors.

Our educational systems do not teach us about these facts and our religions do not teach us about this either. Thoughts are just conditional events that arise in the mind in response to circumstances, and their automatic construction is based on everything we have ever previously experienced that has become a memory. For life we need to learn how to deal with whatever thoughts that arise within us. We need to learn how to think accurately and usefully as well as focus on those thoughts that move us in positive directions without getting caught up in negativity. In fact, we need to learn how to silence or disempower the negative thought afflictions that accost us. One can call the mastery of these wanted mental skills the pursuit or cultivation of wisdom.

The Confucian way to do this is to work on polishing your mind and behavior. To elevate your behavior you are to watch your internal mental tableau and then cut off errant thoughts along with the wrong words or behaviors they lead to, while remaining natural all the while. In essence you self-edit or self-correct your thoughts and behavior, and you uplift them both by watching your thoughts and elevating them whenever appropriate.

The proper Confucian way is not to become overly rigid, inflexible, sclerotic or ossified about your thoughts and behavior such that rigid rules are established and you lose all adaptability. The proper way does not involve creating a society so rigidly bound by rules – such as seen with the Amish or Orthodox Jewish communities - that people find their culture claustrophobic and oppressive.

In China's past many people made this mistake because they interpreted Confucius incorrectly, creating rigid rules of conduct and teaching that one must never deviate from tradition. In China this ossification destroyed the proper interpretation of Confucius's teachings.

As another warning, ancient Sparta was also destroyed due to a rigid adherence to ancient custom and time-sanctified tradition, which also prevented it from becoming an empire or anything spectacular in fields like philosophy, art or wealth. That adherence prevented her from adapting herself to new ways when necessary and so in defending the old without flexibility, adaptability and the willingness to change she eventually perished.

If you don't feed errant thoughts and desires with energy but abstain from fusing with them they will eventually leave your mind and your mental realm will gradually calm down. This is one way of dealing with thought deviants, and is why you can find inner calm and serenity through the practice of sitting meditation. Meditation teaches a detachment you can carry into the regular world after you practice long enough to develop this skill. With calmness and clarity as your belt you can more easily choose to follow your highest nature, which is the highest of human achievements.

In case you are wondering, this is the actual spiritual pathway of ennoblement, spiritualization and divinization! It all has to do with perfecting your mind and behavior, but the pathway requires practice and effort. Spiritualization doesn't just happen. It requires self-work. You become more refined by gradually eliminating the faults and flaws you discover in yourself. You can only become an exemplary person, and then sage, by slowly stripping yourself of flawed ways you have picked up and practiced so many years.

When you cannot detach from thoughts that seem to impel you with pressure so that you often succumb to bad behavior, you might also try the strategy of distraction to occupy your mind with other activities in order to break any hold that negative thoughts, impulses or desires might have on you. When you can finally learn how to detach from thoughts then your mind will gradually become more quiet and it will enter into a degree of "cessation." Mental independence from getting caught up in your thoughts is what leads to better decisions and better behavior.

As Vedanta says, "If you have no connection with the mind flow, you are out of it. You are apart from it." You must therefore come to recognize that thoughts are just words and pictures that flow through your mind automatically and not the real world. By recognizing them as just objects of experience and by remaining independent from them you can create distance from them, and with distance you won't follow them automatically. If you did act upon every thought, urge or emotion that ever appeared in your brain then you would probably be in jail, wouldn't you? Obviously you need some way to censor them, change them, or detach from those that are inappropriate but won't leave and continue to impel you.

Therefore, you first need awareness to be able to stand back like an independent observer and recognize your thoughts and emotions that are to be ignored since they don't move you in the direction you want to go. This requires a higher independent wisdom of viewing and understanding your thoughts and emotions.

Next you need to learn how to defuse from those recurrent thoughts when they give you pressure so that they are just mental events that come and go rather than pressured commands that control you. You have to cultivate the power to override errant desires, impulses, habits or emotions. Part of that ability comes from the detachment you cultivate via the Confucian way, which is designed to help you purify your mental realm and behavior. This is a non-denominational pathway to cultivating the purity of ennoblement.

The result from doing this in life is the development of a pure mind that is awake, aware, open, balanced and bright. The mind is never to be suppressed (you must always allow your thoughts to arise) but must be tamed in the sense that we need to learn how to use it rightly. It should always remain open and free so that it clearly sees and knows the thoughts within it. Through meditation and mindfulness practice it can become like a clear mirror that reflects thoughts and images clearly but does not stick to them at all.

You should not overly play with negative thoughts when they arise within your mind so that you become stickily entangled with them. A healthy mind either leaves them alone, cuts them off using various skillful means or switches topics to concentrate on something else. As a result of mastering such skills unwanted thoughts will leave your mental realm and stop bothering you. Hence the name of this practice is cessation (thoughts stop or errant behavior ceases) and observation (you witness/watch your thoughts). You cease or stop errant thoughts through observation. By witnessing them without getting snarled inside their complex you can resist getting pulled into their nonsense and they will ultimately leave.

In addition to Confucius, the Christian monk St. Augustine also emphasized this form of mental practice as the road to help you purify your mind and transform your behavior. Only if you watch yourself can you tame yourself, otherwise you won't ever be cognizant of what you are really doing.

Christianity often talks about how man may become God, and *this* method is the technique of spiritualization or divinization. It is the way to pursue mental and behavioral purification. This is why Confucianism, although free of religious connotations and overtones, is often considered a spiritual path for it is also a pathway to the same type of divine perfection – purity in mind and behavior. The Confucian way involves reflection, contemplation, a consistent effort for self-improvement and a devoted participation in society for society.

One of the most famous practitioners of the Confucian way was Yuan Liao Fan, whose Ming dynasty story can be found in *Liao Fan's Four Lessons*. The lessons in *Liao Fan's Four Lessons* on how to change your thoughts, personality, and fated destiny have been so popular that countless copycat versions have appeared over the centuries to promote its teachings. I highly recommend that you read it and also give it to your children to study.

As the story goes, in order to purify his mind and behavior and change his fated fortune, Liao Fan created a ledger of daily merits and demerits that he would constantly update from observing his mind and behavior. This is similar to the practice of various Christian nuns who would attach a small booklet around their waists within which they were to record any improper thoughts they had throughout the day in order to help them eliminate their character faults. Throughout his day Liao Fan similarly practiced mindfulness to watch his mind in order to cut off bad thoughts, create good thoughts in their place, practice good deeds and stop performing bad actions.

As the great Confucian Wang Yang-Ming said, "This effort must be carried out continuously. Like eradicating robbers and thieves, one must resolve to wipe them out completely. In idle moments one must search out and discover each and every selfish thought for sex, wealth, fame and the rest. One must resolve to pluck out and cast away the root of the sickness, so that it can never arise again. Only then may one begin to feel at ease. One must, at all times, be like a cat catching mice – with eyes intently watching and ears intently listening. As soon as a single [selfish] thought begins to stir, one must conquer it and cast it out. Act as if you were cutting a nail in two or slicing through iron. Do not indulge or accommodate it in any way. Do not harbor it, and do not allow it to escape."[2]

Remember that if thoughts will not move you in a proper direction then you must abandon them for better ones. First you have to watch your thoughts to note when they go astray, and then you have to cut off any negative inclinations while replacing them with positive ones. This is how you become a better person, or how you become "better than your (current) self."

Liao Fan, being taught by his teacher, used a unique form of moral arithmetic to help him eliminate bad thoughts and behavior over time. He would watch his mind throughout the day, and at the end of the day kept a journal ledger which recorded a net running sum where one bad thought or bad deed cancelled out one good thought or good deed. Every evening Liao Fan would record his efforts at self-perfection by tallying such results, and then offered the net report to Heaven to show his efforts and progress. At that time he would reflect upon what had happened during the day to help strengthen his truthfulness, sincerity and desire for transforming himself.

His method is similar to the famous practice of the saintly King Kulashekhara of Southern India, who did not consider his kingdom his own but would submit at the end of each working day a report of his court activities to Heaven. Considering himself as a caretaker of the kingdom, he also practiced this mindful self-perfection throughout the day in the service to his country.

The great Chinese emperor Tang Taizong practiced self-perfection a

---

[2] Philip Ivanhoe, *Confucian Moral Self Cultivation* (Hackett Publishing Company, Indianapolis: Illinois, 2000), p. 67.

different way by encouraging officials to speak up against his faults and errors so that their remonstrance could serve as a mirror for self-correction. He knew that power corrupts, so rather than surround himself with yes men he used the judgment of his officials to help keep him away from great error.

This is, by the way, why all modern governments need a free press (the Fourth Estate) to report on their wrongdoings and keep them in line for the public good. A free press insures that a government acts in fairness to its own people. By establishing a transparency where the governed know what their government is doing, it becomes a vehicle that can reduce corruption and correct those in power.

In his autobiography, Liao Fan said that he made a vow to Heaven to perform a certain number of good deeds in order that Heaven might help him change his fated destiny as once foretold to him by an infallible fortune teller. He finally did change his fate because of this daily ledger practice, which helped him avoid the errors that were producing his bad fortune.

Liao Fan's basic formula[3] was to practice Confucian awareness-mindfulness, mantra (asking Heaven for assistance) and merit-making (doing good deeds for others while stopping bad thoughts and deeds) in order to "accumulate the merit" necessary to change his fated destiny. It is said that success in life arises out of the steady accumulation of advantages, but we can also say that your fortune results from the steady accumulation of merit. Liao Fan tried to accumulate a great stock of merit so that he could change his fortune for the better, and mental introspection while pushing himself to do good deeds was the way he chose to do so.

What is merit? Merit is a type of spiritual and material wealth of good fortune you accumulate by doing altruistic deeds on behalf of others so that they benefit. It is a stock of positive karma then owed to you because of doing such good deeds. While Buddhists, Jains, Hindus, Taoists and many other groups believe in karma, so do Confucians because of the teachings within the *Yijing* ("Those who accumulate good deeds will certainly experience an excess of blessings, while those who accumulate bad deeds will experience excess of calamity"). Confucians feel that a family which performs good deeds will accumulate merit and this will, in turn, create for it a better and more prosperous future. This is the concept of karma.

---

[3] Detailed in *Move Forward: Powerful Strategies for Creating Better Outcomes in Life* and *Quick, Fast, Done.*

Many Christians, as another instance, also firmly believe that doing good deeds will win you a place in Heaven, which is basically the principle of karma again. The idea of karma is that doing good deeds will win you wholesome rewards and doing bad deeds will produce an unfortunate future. Some people perform good deeds just because they like doing good deeds, some because they were taught to do good deeds, and some for the additional desire to accumulate merit for its rewards.

Liao Fan classified doing good deeds as cultivating love and respect for other people, loving and cherishing all beings, helping people in desperate need, donating money to good causes, developing public projects for the benefit of the people, helping people succeed in their endeavors, supporting the practice of kindness, persuading others to practice kindness, protecting proper teachings, and respecting elders. These are just a few examples of the many ways in which we might help others and accumulate merit. As Confucius taught, self-cultivation has the ultimate purpose of finding its expression through active helpful participation in the world like this, and that active engagement was to embody a moral commitment to benefiting others through such methods.

Liao Fan's means of Confucian cultivation - his formula for transforming his karmic fate and destiny as told to him from the fortune teller - were taught to him by Zen Master Yungu and left for us in *Liao Fan's Four Lessons*. The whole reason his story came about is because Liao Fan had come to believe that his astrological fortune and destiny for life was absolutely fated. He believed this because it had consistently been predicted with impossible exactitude. No tiny detail of his fate, however improbable the prediction, had ever failed to come true. This included unpredictable things such as even the amount of his salary at various points in his career, his job positions and city postings, and his rank in passing each of several important imperial examinations. Among the predictions for his life, the infallible fortune telling Taoist monk, named Kong, had foretold that Liao Fan would only live to age 53 and never have a son. These are the two events that Liao Fan wanted to change most of all.

Master Yungu met Liao Fan after many incredible predictions had already come true, and taught him how to reform his behavior and change his character so that he could create a new destiny. Master Yungu explained the Confucian teaching that the *Book of Songs* and *Classic of History* both say that a man determines his fate himself and secures good or bad fortune by his own doing. However, while we all create our individual fate from our past actions we then certainly have the ability to change it.

The lesson you will learn from Liao Fan's story is that you must never depend on good fortune arriving from Heaven but must work to create fate yourself, for that is the true pathway of success. When a person's good deeds are incredibly numerous they can truthfully change a destiny from bad to good. They can change suffering to happiness or poverty to prosperity. You can even change the fate of a very short life to experiencing longevity by virtue of doing the right things. But you still have to work at it.

Master Yungu explained to Liao Fan that each man was indeed allotted a given fate or astrological destiny at birth that would determine specific karmic outcomes for his life. This was perfectly true, which is why methods such as astrology work wonderfully when practiced by a skillful master. However, through vigorous action – whether through good or bad deeds – a man can change his allotment of good or bad fortune that is due to transpire in life. This is why both the Chinese and Indian cultures have both methods for predicting fate and remedial measures for bad karma, otherwise what would be the point of predicting fate if it could not be changed?

Master Yungu explained that a man who automatically followed his thoughts, binding to them strongly rather than defusing from them in order to follow higher and better principles, follows the fixed path that is fated to occur due to his own rigidity. This type of individual, who binds with the thoughts that create his future, becomes unable to transcend his destiny to create a new fortune.

How do you transcend destiny? As Master Yungu explained, you must detach from the thoughts, desires, attitudes, emotions, impulses and inclinations that would normally control you and impel you down a fated pathway. The autobiographical story of Liao Fan explains how to do so. This story, taken from *Liao Fan's Four Lessons*, fully illustrates the Confucian way of spirituality, ennoblement and changing a fated destiny:

> Master Yungu asked what were Mr. Kong's predictions regarding my entire life. I honestly told him the whole story (that I would only receive certain imperial appointments, die at a young age and never have a son). He then asked if I felt that I deserve imperial appointments or a son. I reflected upon my

previous deeds and attitudes in the past for a long time. Then I answered him saying, "No, I do not feel that I deserve an imperial appointment or a son. Those who received imperial appointments all had the appearance of good fortune and I do not. I do not work towards accumulating virtues to build up my good fortune either. I am very impatient, intolerant, undisciplined and narrow-minded. I also have a strong sense of pride and arrogance and sometimes show off my intelligence and talent in putting down others. I also behave arbitrarily and speak without any sense of restraint. These are all signs of scant good fortune and virtue. How could I possibly receive an imperial appointment?"

There is an old saying, "Life springs from the dirt of the earth. Clear water often harbors no fish." The first reason why I feel I do not deserve a son is that I am overly attached to cleanliness, resulting in the lack of thoughtfulness for others. The second reason is that I have a quick temper and easily become angry. The third reason is based on the principle that I overly guard my own reputation and cannot sacrifice anything for the sake of others. The fourth reason is that I talk too much which wastes a lot of Qi, or energy. The fifth reason is that I also delight in drinking alcohol and that depletes my spirit. The sixth reason I do not have a son is my habit of staying up nights, not knowing how to conserve my energy. Aside from these, I have many, many, other faults which are too numerous to mention.

Master Yungu then said, "According to you then, there are many things in life you do not deserve, not only fame and a son! Those who have millions of dollars in this life must have cultivated the good fortune worthy of that amount in the past. Those who have thousands of dollars must also have good fortune, which is worthy of generating that sum. Those, who die of starvation were in fact were meant to die in that manner. We must understand that their own past thoughts and actions created the fate of these people; the karmic result today is simply the fruit of their deeds. Heavenly beings do not have any intentions for us.

"Bearing children is similar to bearing fruit from seeds. If the seeds are planted well, the fruits will flourish. If the seeds are not planted well, then the fruits will become malnourished. For example, if a person has accumulated enough merits and virtues for a hundred generations, then he or she will have descendants to last a hundred generations. One who accumulates enough merits and virtues to last ten generations will then have ten generations of descendants to live out that good fortune. The same goes for three generations or two generations. For those who have no descendants at all, it is because they have not accumulated enough good merits and virtues.

"Now that you recognize your own shortcomings, you need to put forth your utmost efforts into working to change and into reforming your misdeeds, which cause you not to have a child or become an imperial official. You would do well to cultivate virtue and tolerance and to treat others with compassion and harmony. Also, care for your health and conserve your energy and spirit.

"Live as though everything of the past dissolved yesterday and all of the future begins today. If you can accomplish this, then you are a person born anew, a person of virtue and sincerity. If even our body is governed by destiny, then how can a body of virtue and sincerity not evoke a response from Heaven?

"As is said in the 'Tai Jia Chapter' of the *Classic of History*, 'One may run away from the decrees of Heaven, but one can never escape the retribution for one's own wrong deeds.' In other words, one can alter the retribution due from past deeds, but if one continues to behave immorally, then there is no chance of avoiding disaster.

"It is also said in the *Book of Songs,* 'People should often reflect upon their own thoughts and actions to see if they accord with the ways of Heaven. If one practices in this way, then good fortune will come without being sought. The choice to seek good fortune or to bring about adversity is all up to the individual.'

"Mr. Kong had predicted that you would not receive an imperial appointment or have a son. We can think of these as the decrees of Heaven, but even that can still be changed. You only need to develop your virtue, diligently try to practice kind deeds and work to accumulate many hidden merits and virtues. These are your own transactions to create good fortune. How is it then possible that you will not get to enjoy them?

"The *Yijing* was written to help people bring about good fortune and avoid adversity. If everything is predestined with no room for change, then how can we improve upon our good fortune and avoid adversity? The very first chapter of the *Yijing* also said, 'Families who often perform kind deeds will have an excess of good fortune to pass on to the next generations.' Do you believe this?"

I replied "Yes."

I understood and believed the Master and gratefully paid my respects to him by prostrating. Then I began to regret all my past wrongdoings, whether large or small, in front of the Buddha's image. I wrote down my wish to pass the imperial examinations and vowed to complete three thousand meritorious deeds to show my gratitude towards ancestors, earth and Heaven.

Upon hearing my vow, Master Yungu showed me a merit-fault chart and taught me how to keep a daily record of all the kind and unkind acts I committed in a day. He told me that bad deeds could neutralize the merits I had accrued from good deeds. The Master also taught me to recite the Zhunti mantra. Only with a pure and concentrated mind could what I seek for come true.

Master Yungu explained, "It is said, 'Those who are considered experts in the art of drawing talismans but do not know the right way to do it will be laughed at by spirits and gods.' The secret behind writing a talisman is the absence of thoughts from start to finish. In the process of drawing, one must not give rise to a single wandering thought; even kind thoughts have to be let go of. Only under these circumstances can drawing a talisman be successful. When one asks for or seeks something in terms of changing one's fate, it is important that one does so with a mind that is clear and empty. In this way, one will easily receive a response.

"Mencius discussed in his 'Principle of Forming Destiny' that, 'There is no difference between a long life and a short life.'

At first glance, one would find this hard to understand. How can long life and short life be the same? In fact, when we do not give rise to thought there is no duality, so there is no difference between a long life and short life. We will see everything with eyes of equality and live morally regardless of good or bad times. If one can practice accordingly, then one can master the fate of wealth and poverty. When we are able to create and form our own destiny, it does not matter whether we are presently rich or poor."

Master Yungu said, "If one can practice morality regardless of conditions, then he or she will surely change a poor life into a prosperous one, and a prosperous life into an even longer lasting prosperity.

"One should also look upon long life and short life equally. A person who knows he or she is short-lived should not think, 'I am going to die anyway, so there is no point in being virtuous. I should steal and kill for my benefit while I can.' One who is long-lived should not think, 'I have all the time in the world. It does not matter if I do something bad once in while.' One who understands this principle will be able to change a short life into a long life through virtuous behavior.

"The most important concern for human beings is that of life and death. So talking about long life and short life (since this is the matter of life and death) encompasses all conditions that apply to wealth and poverty, good or bad reputation, whether favorable or unfavorable, whether gain or loss.

"One who wishes to cultivate needs to do so daily and to be mindful of his or her conduct every moment, ensuring that no transgressions are made. We have to wait until our cultivation reaches a certain level and then our destiny will change. This change depends on the accumulation of merits, and on seeking a response from Heaven. When cultivating, one needs to be aware of one's own faults and resolve to correct them just as in curing a sickness.

"Perseverance is required and attainment comes when one's practice matures and ripens. In that case, one's destiny will most definitely change for the better. We should work toward severing all bad habits and thoughts. It would be quite an accomplishment in cultivating these teachings to be able to reach the innate state of 'no thought.' It is the actual learning and practice of wisdom.

"The actions of worldly people usually follow their thoughts. Whatever has to be 'thought' is not considered natural. I know that you are still unable to accomplish the state of 'no thought,' but if you practice reciting the Zhunti mantra continuously, it will help you to overcome scattered thoughts. When you recite, you must not think of reciting, but recite consciously and diligently without any attachment. When the reciting becomes second nature, it will be effective."

Liao-Fan said, "My name used to be Xue-Hai, which meant 'broad learning,' but after receiving these teachings from Master Yungu, I changed it to Liao-Fan, which means 'transcending the ordinary.' It signified my understanding of the fact that we create our destiny and that I did not wish to be like worldly people, who allowed destiny to control them."

From then on, I began to be very cautious and careful in whatever I thought or did. Soon I felt quite different from before. In the past, I used to be careless and lived my days in distraction and had no self-discipline at all. Now, I found myself being naturally cautious and conscientious in my thoughts, speech and actions. I maintain this attitude even when I am alone, for I know that there are spirits and gods everywhere who can see my every action and thought. Even when I encounter people, who dislike or slander me, I can take their insults with a patient and peaceful mind and not feel compelled to quarrel with them.

The year after I met Master Yungu, I took the preliminary imperial exam in which Mr. Kong had predicted I would come in third place. Amazingly, I came in first! Mr. Kong's predictions were beginning to lose their accuracy. He had not predicted I would pass the imperial exam at all, but that autumn, I did! None of these were part of my original destiny. Master Yungu had said that destiny can be changed. And now I believe it more than ever! Although I had corrected many of my faults, I found that I could not wholeheartedly do the things I ought to do. Even if I did do them, it was forced and unnatural. I reflected within and found that I still had many shortcomings.

Sometimes I forced myself to act kindly, but my speech was still untamed and offensive. I found I could contain myself when sober, but after a few drinks I would lose self-discipline and act without restraint. Although I often practiced kind deeds and accumulated merits, my faults and offenses were so numerous, they seemed to outnumber my good deeds. A lot of my time was spent vainly and without value. It took me more than ten years to complete the three thousand meritorious deeds I had vowed to do.

I was not able to dedicate the merits from these three thousand kind deeds at a temple until I returned to my hometown in the south a few years later. Then I made my second wish and that was for a son. I vowed to complete another three thousand good deeds. A few years later, your mother gave birth to a boy and named him Tian-Chi.

Every time I performed a kind deed, I would record it in a book. Your mother, who could not read or write, would use a goose feather dipped in ink and make a red circle on the calendar for every kind deed she did. Sometimes she gave food to the poor or bought living creatures from the marketplace to free in the wild. She recorded all of these with her circles on the calendar. At times, she could accumulate more than ten red circles in one day!

Everyday we practiced like this and in four years, the three thousand deeds were completed. Again, I made the dedications, this time in our home. On September thirteenth of that same year, I made my third wish and that was to pass the next level of the imperial examination, the Jinshr level. I also vowed to complete ten thousand meritorious deeds. After three years, I attained my wish and passed the Jinshr level. I was also made the mayor of Baodi province. While in that office, I prepared a small book to record my merits and faults, and called it "The Book of Disciplining the Mind."

From that day, I recorded all my good and bad deeds in that book and kept it on my desk. Every evening, I would burn incense and make a report of my deeds to the heavens at the little altar in the garden.[4]

This, in short, is the method that Liao Fan used to purify his mind, upgrade his behavior and thereby change his fortune. He transcended his fate by accumulating merit through reducing his faults that were leading him astray. By policing his mind and behavior he was able to create a new fate that was much better, but all of this took time and effort. If you want to change your fate and fortune, you must accept the fact that it will require a continuous push toward self-improvement, and then get on with it.

All achievement, whether to achieve a success in life already fated or to achieve a success in defiance of fate, requires effort. This means a gritty perseverance or "never give up" attitude of pursuit and endurance. In the case of mentally watching ourselves we can say that vigilance has its limits because attention grows tired and mental guards go down, so Liao Fan created a ledger recording system for his efforts to help catch himself in any acts of wrongdoing and keep himself on track.

Benjamin Franklin

The American hero Benjamin Franklin also practiced a similar form of Confucian introspection in order to eliminate his character flaws and take on the task of cultivating virtue. Franklin was a man who rose from nothing, who gained no advantages from parentage or patronage and who enjoyed no advantages of an early education, but became one of the greatest Americans of achievement known to history. He credited a particular method of self-observation with helping him build his character. He used it to develop a garden of virtues and excellences that made him both more effective in life and endearing to others, and this helped him achieve much of his success and happiness in life.

Franklin explained in his autobiography that on a daily basis, just like Liao Fan, he would mentally watch his own behavior and police himself against committing thirteen different types of non-virtuous acts. His method can also easily be emulated by any individual who wishes to change their thoughts, attitudes, habits, character, personality or behaviors.

Either method, or some new method constructed from their

---

[4] Liao-Fan Yuan, *Liao-Fan's Four Lessons* (Buddha Dharma Education Association, Taiwan).

similarities, can be used by anyone who wishes to pursue a pathway of great accomplishment or self-perfection. Since they are similar to sports training techniques, you can also vary these basic methods in various ways to create your own technique for self-perfection or self-accomplishment. First you must decide upon an ideal you want to strive for, and then you can use some version of these techniques to get there from here.

The specialness of Franklin's method was that he chose to focus on mastering only one virtue per week – either temperance ("eat not to dullness, drink not to elevation"), silence ("speak not but what may benefit others or yourself; avoid trifling conversation"), order ("let all your things have their places"), resolution ("resolve to perform what you ought; perform without fail what you resolve"), frugality ("waste nothing"), industry ("lose not time; be always employed in something useful"), sincerity ("use no hurtful deceit"), justice ("wrong none by doing injuries"), moderation ("avoid extremes"), cleanliness ("tolerate no uncleanness in body, clothes or habituation"), tranquility ("be not disturbed at trifles, or at accidents common or unavoidable"), chastity ("rarely use sex but for health or offspring, never to the injury of your own or another's peace or reputation") and humility ("imitate Jesus and Socrates"). While Liao Fan was looking to decrease every type of fault at once, Franklin chose to concentrate on eliminating just one type of fault per week.

The number of virtues one might cultivate is always a personal mater, but in *Analects* 17.6 Confucius suggested that humans focus on cultivating five traits of character: "People who can put into practice five things in the broader world can be considered consummate in their conduct." When his student Zigong asked what were the five, Confucius answered respectfulness, magnanimity (so that you can influence others), being true to one's word (so that others can depend on you), a nimble mind (which allows you to succeed) and generosity.

Christianity suggests seven virtues – chastity or purity (abstinence), temperance (equanimity), charity (benevolence, generosity or sacrifice), diligence or persistence, patience (forgiveness or mercy), kindness (compassion), and humility or modesty. Buddhism espouses ten - generosity, morality, renunciation, wisdom, diligent effort, tolerance or patience, honesty, resolute determination, loving-kindness or goodwill friendliness, and serenity. Other religions propose other cardinal virtues to cultivate, so what you decide to work upon if you choose this method should depend upon your own faults and higher objectives.

Franklin wrote in his autobiography, "I judg'd it would be well not to distract my attention by attempting (to perfect) the whole at once, but to fix it on one of them at a time." Accordingly, for an entire week he paid very strong attention to cutting down any offenses against a single chosen virtue while allowing a normal (but somewhat elevated) attitude to infractions against the other virtues he had also wanted to perfect. Unlike Liao Fan who monitored everything evenly, Franklin considered himself a gardener who was removing weeds from one of thirteen flower beds at a time, and who was scheduled to return to repeat the course again after twelve weeks with each time pass expecting to find fewer weeds amidst the flowers. Weeding out his faults in this way may seem like a trivial affair not worth the effort, but perfecting the mundane details of life and conduct are what contribute significantly to the formation of one's character.

The inherent idea behind Franklin's technique, or Liao Fan's methodology for self-change and merit accumulation, was that you have to become conscious of yourself, watch your mind, and give self-policing your full attention if you want to truly change in any way. Just saying you want to change is not enough. The results of this process will not necessarily be quick, but in time with its application there will definitely be more clarity in your thinking and purity in your behavior. By restricting your focus and attention to improving just one aspect of your character per week you are more likely to be successful at achieving positive results in behavioral change.

Franklin's method mirrors modern psychological findings that those who try to make big changes in their life usually fail if they try to do too much at once. People normally must scale down big desires to focus on smaller objectives that are achievable. To become successful at character development, you have to recognize that becoming a better person is a gradual process of moral development that heavily depends on a steady accumulation of simple acts rather than a grand burst of goodness.

Franklin admittedly wrote that by initially trying to monitor and change all his faults at once, "While my care was employ'd in guarding against one fault, I was often surprised by another. Habit took the advantage of inattention; inclination was sometimes too strong for reason." This is why he developed a gradual course to virtue that was divided into thirteen weeks with a special emphasis on just one virtue every seven days.

Consider that those people who want to simultaneously quit smoking, drinking, substance abuse or overeating usually *fail at all of them* because they place too many simultaneous demands on their self-control. Willpower then fails them, as does their commitment to attentive watching and concentration. Only when they reduce their consumption a little at a time do they usually succeed, as Franklin suggested.

Liao Fan treated all his misconduct equally, but Franklin's efforts to cultivate virtue were more focused and concentrated. However, they did not put an emphasis on doing good deeds to accumulate merit, which is a fantastic part of Liao Fan's system. Franklin did that separate from this system. Nonetheless, both of their systems involved cultivating attention to one's thoughts and behavior. Both systems also involved a recording system of feedback so that progress could be honestly monitored and measured. Both realized that without honest, accurate feedback (measurement or monitoring recorded in a ledger-based system) neither would be able to determine whether or not they were actually making progress. Without a progress measuring system they would not be able to determine whether they were doing something right or wrong, how they were falling short or doing well, and where they needed to improve.

In *How I Raised Myself From Failure to Success in Selling*, ex-major league baseball player turned insurance salesman Frank Bettger decided to take Franklin's method and adapt it for business pursuits. As a result of his adapted technique, he became one of the most outstanding salesmen in his company, achieving *both material and psychological goals*. This is something to take note of, which is the fact that this basic technique can be used to help you attain worldly goods and accomplishments rather than just character virtues. If you want to excel in business success you might consider using it.

As stated, many Christian monks and nuns also practiced a similar mindfulness technique by carrying around a notebook attached to their waist, using it to record all infractions against mental purity or proper behavior during the day. The method has even been used in Tibetan Buddhism because it embodies the basic technique of mindfully watching your mind for faults, and then cutting them off whenever you see them.

As previously mentioned, the great benefit of the Confucian technique used by Liao Fan and Benjamin Franklin is that their infractions were recorded on paper, thus formalizing their efforts and thus increasing their effectiveness. We already know about Liao Fan's exact methodology whereas we didn't reveal Franklin's exactly. It is as follows: "I made a little book, in which I allotted a page for each of the virtues. I rul'd each page with red ink, so as to have seven columns, one for each day of the week, marking each column with a letter for the date. I cross'd these columns with thirteen red lines, on which line, and in its proper column, I might mark, by a little black spot, every fault I found upon examination to have been committed respecting that virtue upon that day.

"I determined to give a week's strict attention to each of the virtues successively. Thus, in the first week, my great guard was to avoid every the least offense against Temperance, leaving the other virtues to their ordinary chance, only marking every evening the faults of the day. Thus, if in the first week I could keep my first line, marked T, clear of spots, I suppos'd the habit of that virtue so much strengthen'd, and its opposite weaken'd, that I might venture extending my attention to include the next, and for the following week keep both lines clear of spots. Proceeding thus to the last, I could go thro' a course compleat in thirteen weeks, and four courses in a year. And like him who, having a garden to weed, does not attempt to eradicate all the bad herbs at once, which would exceed his reach and his strength, but works on one of the beds at a time, and, having accomplish'd the first, proceeds to a second, so I should have, I hoped, the encouraging pleasure of seeing on my pages the progress I made in virtue, by clearing successively my lines of their spots, till in the end, by a number of courses, I should be happy in viewing a clean book, after a thirteen weeks' daily examination."

Franklin's daily record of his progress provided a means of positive feedback on measuring the effectiveness of his efforts. By recording his progress on paper it forced him to admit where mistakes were continually being made in inhibitory control. Writing things down allowed him to examine his track record, whose daily review motivated him to constantly improve on his personal best to become better than himself. As Mencius said, "Those who follow what is great within them become great; those who follow what is small become small."

Franklin's daily record employs the principle of "measurement ends argument" because measuring things allows you to know if you are improving or not. If you don't measure things to know where you stand, how can you take the right steps to improve your behavior? Franklin and Liao Fan each reviewed the day's cultivation record on a nightly basis so that their progress was monitored.

Another saying runs, "people respect what they measure." If you use either of these methods of self-improvement or some variation thereof and submit to the formal discipline of nightly review (where you "report your progress to Heaven") you are sure to elevate your behavior because looking at the track record will motivate you to improve upon it.

Just as in sports, only dedicated commitment to supervised training can drive you to make elevating changes in your behavior. It doesn't require a commitment to religion, but few can develop an extraordinary purity of behavior without the structural guidance offered by a religious path. This is why you must use these special efforts revealed by Liao Fan and Ben Franklin, or some variant that is equally effective. In *Analects* 1.4 Confucius's student Zengzi stated that he used a version of this technique for he said, "I examine my personal conduct every day in three ways. First, in my interactions with others, have I done all that I can? Second, when dealing with friends and peers, have I managed to keep my word? Finally, have I received and acted upon what I learned?"

The right sort of self-reflective and self-corrective practice carried out over time always leads to self-improvement. Lectures on good behavior do not. This type of technique is the only thing that does.

The self-observational method of vigilant mindfulness has a set of general principles upon which various alternative methods, such as Liao Fan's, Franklin's, Bettger's and Zengzi's, are all based. Many individuals have found that various derivatives of these awareness-mindfulness practices - such as ACT or cognitive therapy - have helped them change their lives and fortunes in a most positive way. Just as people gradually learn how to do things that were not previously possible, through these methods they can step-by-step learn how to elevate their behavior to separate themselves from their lower nature. This pursuit of consummate behavior is what produces the noble person and eventually the sage, which is why Confucius called this the Great Learning.

What is the Great Learning in life? To understand this we must first recognize that China has three great religions – Taoism, Buddhism and Confucianism. Taoism feels that the Great Learning is to realize the Tao (achieve enlightenment), cultivate the Tao (use all your enlightenment capabilities) and prove the teachings of the Tao. Buddhism says you are to enlighten yourself, help enlighten other people and enlighten your mind and behavior perfectly, meaning that your actions should exhibit compassionate action consummately joined with wisdom. Confucius said that Great Learning involves enlightening yourself as to the potential of pristine awareness or pure consciousness (cultivating bright virtue), being kind to all people (loving and teaching the people and working for them), and working to reach a final state of pure virtue.

How does a Confucian go about cultivating the Great Learning? Through meditation practice and the daily mindfulness process of self-reflection and self-correction. Both Confucius and Zengzi both said that this process of self-observation - which we now call self-reflection, self-policing or introspection - works better if we make it a daily process just as Liao Fan and Franklin stressed. Vigilant mindfulness or self-reflection will help us guide our thinking and behavior to higher octaves, but only if we do so regularly. As Confucius made clear in *Analects* 14.42, you should "Cultivate in yourself respectful attentiveness."

Confucius also said in *Analects* 14.23, "Exemplary people reach higher, petty people descend lower." In other words, we have to make this higher commitment work in our own lives otherwise we are just moving text around in our heads about proper behavior rather than actually becoming better people. We cannot develop virtues by simply talking or thinking about them. They are actualized through repeated practice so you cultivate them by regularly expressing them. You have to have real commitment to them becoming part of your life rather than remaining just thoughts in your head. An ethical, moral, virtuous life is about having a willful personal commitment to better behavior that you self-police, self-correct and self-improve.

You cannot magically act in the world in a better way simply by studying texts about virtue and ethics. You have to establish new habits. You have to become committed to exemplifying virtuous wisdom in outer conduct. You have to rise up and use what you know to become the sunshine that you want others to see. For instance, in *Analects* 13.5 Confucius said, "If people can recite the three hundred passages in the *Book of Songs* yet still fail to make use of that knowledge when given a government position or when sent abroad on diplomatic missions, then what is the use of their studying? Even though they may have learned so much, what is the use of it to them?" Only if you use what you know has personal study been worthwhile, and only if you do what is right do you become a virtuous person.

Countless religions teach us some of the many reasons why you ascend higher from cultivating more self-awareness. For instance, cultivating mental purity through this method while pushing yourself to do good deeds stirs the Qi within your body. Yang Qi arises within you due to meditation, as well as in response to doing good deeds and acting ethically. When this Qi arises in your body it starts to open up your Qi channels, including those within the spine leading to the brain and within the brain.

The frictionless circulation of Qi within you benefits your health and longevity. It also contributes to the preservation of your spirit in the afterlife since it strengthens the cohesiveness of your internal Qi body – the subtle energy substrate of your physical body - that becomes your deva body after death. The stronger the cohesiveness of your inner Qi body from these efforts, which you can improve through spiritual Qi cultivation methods such as meditation, the better the quality of your body in the hereafter.

In order to enhance the cohesiveness of people's subtle bodies, enlightened beings interact with the Qi of human beings all the time in order to help them. The reason for the intervention is to strengthen their Qi and help them open their Qi channels. They often put people through - or make opportune use of - strong emotional experiences of great yin (ex. fear and anxiety or worry) and great yang (ex. joy or ambition) to flood people's inner subtle bodies with higher levels of yin Qi or yang Qi, thus strengthening them everywhere so that they function better during life and last longer after death.

As the Qi channels of the nervous system become clear of obstructions due to the resultant Qi enervation from meditation and virtuous behavior, over time consciousness then becomes more quiet and clear because of better flowing energy. Watching your mind's mental activities therefore becomes much easier and more natural, and your awareness seems to become brighter because wandering thoughts die out and distractions disappear. Troublesome, distracting or afflictive thoughts decrease, but you still need to learn how to deal with thoughts properly.

This is the gist of spiritual training, is it not? Is it not all about purifying our minds and our behavior? Isn't it about elevating or bettering our minds and how we act in the world to handle experiences and interact with others? When you strip away everything superstitious or supernatural, all the world's spiritual paths come down to the task of divinizing our minds and our behaviors, which are controlled by our minds. The problem or challenge is that we tend to give ourselves over to animalistic tendencies or calculated self-interest instead.

How do we divinize or spiritualize our minds? The mind is the seat of our consciousness, and sentience is the highest ability of a living being. Spirituality therefore entails learning how to use the mind (consciousness) in the highest way possible, for the mind is the ruler of behavior. Fix the mind – purify it - and you fix behavior. Learn how to deal with your thoughts and you learn how to control your mind. Learn how to create the ones you need/want and ignore the ones you don't and then you elevate your ordinary mental realm.

The path of spirituality therefore entails mastering your mind – dealing skillfully with the thoughts and emotions that arise automatically within it, some of which we don't want (but which won't seem to go away), and how to generate or remain focused on intentional thoughts that *we do want* in order to accomplish any tasks that we want accomplished.

Spirituality comes down to how to master (a) the conscious reasoning process, intentional thought generation process and other functional capacities of the mind (attention, mental image making, concentration, intention, distinguishing discrimination, etc.) and (b) automatic processes of the mind such as habits, attitudes and emotions that simply arise. Spirituality is a process of self-improvement or self-mastery because it ultimately involves training your mind to master your thoughts and emotions, and from there your body (its movements and internal energy) and behavior. You can master your behavior only if you master your thoughts and automatic habit energies. This is the key to mastering your body *and its internal energies* too.

Part of mastering your mind involves mastering concentration and focus so that your mental realm is not always haphazardly scattered with wild content so that it is unable to accomplish anything. Concentration entails pursuing focus and mental stability, which entails not paying attention to random, wandering or distracting thoughts while holding onto the thoughts you want.

Mastering your mind also entails mastering a specific capability little discussed, namely how to use it to control your internal energy and move it in various ways inside your body for specific purposes. Your Qi and consciousness are linked, so this capability is something we all have that only needs to be developed through practice. This is what cultivation schools such as Yoga, Taoism and Vajrayana teach.

Mastering your mind also entails mastering your physical body, such as learning how to move it in various excellent ways for dance, athletic sport, when you are trying to be persuasive, and so forth.

Mastering your mind involves perfecting your outer behavior, including the task of establishing virtuous relationships with people and the environment. It also involves mastering external skills (such as fishing, skiing, flying a plane, using a computer program, etc.) and the ability to accomplish things, like knowing how to organize and manage people.

The spiritualization of our mind so that it rises as far as possible above the realm of the animals entails how to properly use thoughts, namely how to relate to them as well as how to gain skills from mastering our thoughts and emotions and their expression into behavior. The spiritualization of our mind entails *cultivating the capabilities and functions of a rational mind while transcending the influences of the irrational mind and emotions.* A first step is to start training yourself to witness your mind's doings so that you can gradually develop a detached independent wisdom for dealing with the contents of your mind.

The mind is a vehicle that creates our thoughts and behavior, so purifying its contents of incorrect mental objects and wild randomness while learning how to use it in the highest possible manner *is the true road of spirituality.* What else could it be? These goals on how to use the mind correctly might seem mundane, but are actually what the path of spirituality is all about.

A truly empty mind absent of thoughts is essentially non-aware or insentient. Therefore the true path of spirituality is not about pursuing having no thoughts, but learning how to use the mind correctly and master all its possible functions. A spiritual "mind of purity" is not totally empty of thoughts. Rather, it is a quieter and clearer mind than untrained consciousness that predominantly gives birth to virtuous thoughts. Using the mind correctly, because of the wisdom of proper judgment, is also "a mind of correctness" or "mind of purity."

Spirituality thus entails learning how to ignore distracting thoughts or emotions (especially how to detach from emotions), how to focus and concentrate for long periods of time, how to effectively shift the focus of your attention from one perspective to another, how to set aside short-term gratification for longer-term goals, how to perform long-term planning, how to persevere with tenacity and grit (zeal and hard work) through difficulty and failure, and more.

Spirituality entails learning how to develop analytical mental skills and how to think inductively, deductively, heuristically and dialectically. It involves learning how to understand cause and effect relationships, how to use the rules of logic and inference so as not to be ruled by emotions or jump to conclusions, and learning how to handle ambiguity and manage risks (probabilities). It entails a commitment to reasoning and questioning, and a demand for logical justification of opinions and positions. Spirituality should add intellectual consistency to your life, and entails becoming a critical free thinker.

Spirituality entails learning how to discern between the true and false, how to tell right from wrong, how to seek truth from facts rather than from dogma or ideology, how to distinguish between the important and unimportant, and it involves knowing the difference between proper and improper behavior. It entails learning how to make good judgments and proper decisions, learning how to form models of expectations and learning how to recognize distortions in your thoughts so that you can form better opinions without bias. Being shrewd or astute is actually a characteristic of spirituality because that is wisdom.

Spirituality must focus on people's livelihoods by emphasizing practical, down-to-earth solutions and tangible benefits for humanity rather than supernatural promises that cannot be proved. It must emphasize cooperation between human beings where people work together for the public welfare of all members of society, for it is coordinated cooperation that builds society and holds it together. Societies are a mixture of self-centered and group-centered activities and spirituality must address both of these aspects.

Spirituality entails learning how to create moral values, moral emotions, moral reasoning, moral behavioral capacity and moral willpower. It involves the practice of ethics, morality and virtuous conduct in body and mind. It entails getting along with other people (working with others) in positive relationships, accepting responsibility and remaining accountable for your actions. It entails mastering self-discipline, learning how to change undesired habits and behaviors, learning how to identify needed personality traits and turn them into habits, and learning how to become a lifelong learner who can achieve mastery of any skills you want to acquire.

All these skills, and more, simply enable you to use your mind rightly and to fullest flavor, which thereby separates you greatly from the realm of the animals. This is what spiritual ascension is all about. When developing these skills you don't just uplift yourself from the realm of the animals but also elevate yourself from the realm of ordinary human beings. Mastering the mind in these ways *is* the road of the sages.

Your thoughts control your words, physical body movements, internal energy (once trained) and your behavior so the path of spirituality entails learning how to properly use your mind to gain control of all these functions. Even when you make mistakes, but arrived at those thoughts or actions using the highest methods possible, you have actualized the spiritual way. Spirituality is learning how to use all the capabilities of the mind without falling into lower pathways (such as being controlled by animalistic emotions and impulses).

The spiritual path of transcendence, the pathway of the sages, is to exhibit through your actions the highest values of humanity consistent with wisdom, rationality, empiricism, or however else you wish to word "clear and proper thinking." We also call this the path of consummate behavior. When you have done your absolute best to use all your mental skills to arrive at the ethical decision "this is the right thing to do" and then do it, you have embodied the spiritual way even when you make an error in judgment. Another way of putting it is that virtue or spirituality consists in using the correct, highest or best reasoning and wisdom possible to guide your actions and behavior even if they come out wrong at times. Spirituality doesn't mean you are always perfect, but using the best you know.

The spiritual life should be known as a life of the highest ethics and reasoning that can be maintained independent of any circumstances. This is what separates us from the animals. Ethics and highest reasoning characterizes the best of humanity and leads to the best results in all affairs. Therefore once again, seen from this angle, mastering your mind with all its various facets and functions is the true road of spirituality. Nothing is higher.

One must acquire knowledge and skills for life, but the spiritual path is how to properly use the mind in general. For instance, in *Analects* 9.8 Confucius asked, "Do I have great knowledge of anything? No, I do not.

Yet if a simple rustic asks me a question and I have no answer, I will pursue it from beginning to end until I have gained deeper insight." Through this lesson Confucius taught us how to use our minds properly – when we don't know something we must use all our facilities to work hard to figure it out, researching matters by going to the core of the problem and tracing things back to their causal roots to seek answers. This is the practical way of learning through investigation, and being above the animals this is also the human way or spiritual way.

When we meditate the Qi channels within our body start to open and when we use our mind rightly in virtuous ways they open as well. As more and more Qi channels open within your body you will also fill with vitality and become healthier because your Qi can then flow more freely everywhere. The fact that your Qi channels become less obstructed and fill with flowing Qi helps to eliminate latent sicknesses within your body too, which is why meditation helps to produce many spontaneous cures of illness. This naturally leads to better health and longevity, and it all comes about due to the practice of self-watching. Naturally if you stretch your muscles through exercise and practice inner energy work you can reach supreme heights through this route too.

As stated, by cultivating a mental purity via meditation, and by establishing the habit of mindfully witnessing/watching your thoughts and behavior, you can avoid many behaviors and blunders that would result in negative fortunes. Confucius taught this while Liao Fan and Benjamin Franklin proved it. Meditation and mindfulness will help you change the automatic behaviors of your mind that produce errors and stand in the way of self-perfection! Trying to perfect your mental and outer behaviors is definitely the pathway of spiritualization.

For instance, with greater awareness you might be able to resist a temptation to yell at someone in anger and avoid permanently poisoning a relationship. That mindfulness can help you keep your job whereas expressing anger might lose it. Such a simple example proves that you become a higher human being simply by transcending normal emotional responses. Thus the path of cultivating meditation and good deeds leads to a clear mind, the accumulation of merit, the ability to change your fortune, a healthier body, longevity and even spiritual progress.

This is the pathway for the individual, but also for society as a whole. For society to reach transcendence Confucius not only advised that individuals devote themselves to ethics but that society as a whole practice proper behavior, which Confucianism called the rites or rituals. How can we encourage this? Through various yearly gatherings to renew the sense of spirit in society. Most people think that Confucius over-emphasized rituals in life, but fail to perceive that their purpose is simply to pose a means of ethical aspiration.

Taken rightly, the purpose of state rituals, such as public ceremonies and holidays, is to help uplift and unite society so that people feel more solidly connected. They help to inspire people and allow them a rare opportunity to directly touch a larger spirit in a transcendent fashion. They help to coalesce cooperative and moral value-based societies. They help create stronger bonds of safety and trust where people feel connected and close to one another (even if just temporarily) due to belonging to a mutual identity that shares in a joint future.

Confucius emphasized state rituals because of their ability to form cooperative national unity and embed higher spiritual aspirations within a nation. They can take man further and further away from his animal nature by refining his behavior and uplifting his emotions to a sense of purity or greatness that involves a larger whole.

Sometimes people can feel a sense of "lift," elevation, transcendence, sublimity or even glorification at such events which greatly enriches their lives for the better. These feelings can help to promote the group and unify its bonds since people know it originates within the group. When people partake of such get-togethers and celebrations they want the benefit of feeling that they are (1) close or united, (2) safe or protected and (3) have a joint shared future (an aspiration). Thus rightly employed they can be used to help unite societies.

Many individuals might not otherwise encounter these uplifting and unifying emotions if they didn't come together during national holidays and celebrations. This is why "state rituals" such as national celebrations and holidays are not to be despised. They have the potential for great unifying influences to bind together communities and countries. Cooperation, after all, is the main thing that societies are involved with because in societies people must work together to produce the public goods that benefit all. Countries live or die based on the strength of their national cohesion, and such events are the symbols of national unity. Thus everything possible should be done to increase the cooperative nature within societies and countries by promoting greater cohesion.

Self-reflection helps man on a daily basis cultivate personal purity and greatness of behavior, as well as altruistic cooperation with others, but those results belong to the individual. However, the rites, rituals, holidays or ceremonies held at yearly junctures pertain to society as well as the individual, helping to build cooperative relationships among the people. They are the means for helping to transform a nation as a whole to a better state of being. They not only shape the character of those who practice them but serve the overarching goal of helping to produce on a large-scale the particular set of attitudes and dispositions needed for a peaceful, meaningful, flourishing society. A Confucian cultivates personal virtue through reasoning (wisdom), growing strong relationships, and by *minimizing the negative* while recognizing that these processes can be achieved at the national level too if approached in certain ways.

Confucius once explained that if you simply governed a people by laws then the people would obey them to stay out of jail, but this would do nothing to change their moral nature. However, "Guide the people by virtue and align them with *li* (social norms of conduct, a sense of propriety, personal deportment and behavior), the people will develop a sense of right or wrong and have standards to follow" (*Analects* 2.3). Is this not transforming a nation and the road of spirituality as well?

CHAPTER 7:
CULTIVATING YOUR QI

Mencius clearly mentioned the existence of our internal vital energy, Qi, that is the equivalent of the Prana of India and "wind element" of Buddhism. In these spiritual traditions and others, practitioners are taught to cultivate their Qi in order to transform their bodies and attain enlightenment, which is the equivalent of becoming a sage.

Without going into the specific techniques, which are found everywhere within Chinese culture (especially within the Taoist tradition), the Hindu Yoga schools and Vajrayana,[5] we must note that Mencius taught us that Qi cultivation should be considered an essential part of your self-cultivation routine. Inner Qi cultivation is not alien to the Confucian way.

To become an exemplary (or even "spiritual") human being you must not only practice mindfulness to purify your mind, words and behavior but must also cultivate your body. Specifically, you must cultivate both your physical body and your internal energy, or Qi. This is imperative. A cardinal tenant of Confucian cultivation is to protect your body, which includes the task of preserving it and *cultivating it*, in order that you create a more suitable vehicle for becoming a sage. Cultivating your Qi leads to health along with its traditional benefit of producing better mental states.

There is no way that you can purify your mental realm and reach a mental state of crisp, clear (empty) clarity - often called no-thought, emptiness or pure awareness - without opening up the Qi channels within

---

[5] See *Nyasa Yoga* by William Bodri.

your brain and nervous system. The idea of cultivating pristine awareness and an observant mirror mind, wherein you can clearly know the thoughts of your mind without sticking to then, is championed within Confucianism, Christianity, Vedanta, Sufism, Buddhism and many other spiritual schools because it *is* the pathway of spiritual cultivation. This *is* the means of purifying consciousness, becoming a better human being, and transcending the normal human mentality. This is the road of human ennoblement which separates us from the animals as well as our lower passions. This is the pathway of spiritualization, theosis or divinization. This is what liberates you from the mind, and thus helps you transcend the realm of human existence.

Spiritual cultivation actively stimulates your Qi. Your energized Qi, in turn, affects the Qi channels of your body. Those channel pathways within every cell of your flesh (akin to atomic bonds) naturally become cleared of obstructions when your Qi is activated and starts moving within you.

Because the Confucian way is influenced by the philosophy of the *Yijing* which advises that we learn how to take command of the changes of phenomena and master any processes of transformation, learning how to master the Qi of our body through various exercises, including pranayama, fits in perfectly well with these principles. We must master our mind and behavior through willpower, and we must also learn how to use our willpower to master our internal energy, flooding it everywhere within us. We must perform daily exercises to guide it everywhere within our bodies, flooding all our flesh and bones in order to transform each and every cell of our body.

This is how you create the initial spiritual body. Basically, you strengthen an already existent underlying Qi-substrate within your body, which normally leaves upon death as your spirit body, until it becomes strong enough that it can leave its physical cage at your will.

It is unfortunate that many sages of yore did not emphasize this aspect of the sagely path, which takes twelve years of ardent effort after the real Yang Qi (kundalini) of the body is finally awakened through such daily efforts. In fact, however, even the Zen school, which emphasizes mental cultivation, will tell you that you must cultivate the Qi of your body through various exercises in order to transform your body and succeed at spiritual cultivation. The Esoteric school of Buddhism (Vajrayana) also clearly says you can cultivate mental cleanliness (emptiness) all you want, but without also cultivating your Qi energy you cannot become a sage in 10,000 eons. Taoism is founded upon this principle of inner energy work too.

Since Confucius advised students to master charioteering and archery, which are the equivalents of modern sport (that are also potential warfare preparations), we can understand that the Confucian path is not simply one of quiet sitting meditation and mental watching. It is a practical pathway of active development, and this practicality extends to mastering your internal energy as well.

Mencius explained that your Qi is your internal vital energy, it can be controlled by your willpower, and it can be cultivated to such a degree that it becomes greater. Along these lines he said, "This Qi is extremely large and extremely powerful. Nourish it with righteousness and protect it from harm and it will fill Heaven and Earth. It grows through the accumulation of righteousness and cannot be obtained by contrived actions. If one's actions are not satisfying to one's mind then it shrivels up." This is yet another reason why Confucius said that you must remain faithful to moral behavior. Without a commitment to virtue it is hard to cultivate your Qi properly, and certainly impossible to create an independent spiritual body.

According to Confucian teachings, as well as those of other spiritual schools, our Qi is actually nourished through the steady accumulation of virtuous acts. This explains Mencius's comment. Doing good deeds and practicing the virtues always transforms our Qi in a positive fashion, purifying its impure nature. For instance, when you perform a good deed you often feel warmth within your body because that virtuous deed, however small, affects your Qi in a positive fashion. The warmth signifies having done an auspicious deed and arises because your Qi stirs in response and starts opening up your body's Qi pathways.

All types of selfless ethical deeds performed with others in mind, such as acts of charity, move or purify your Qi in beneficial ways. This activation actually opens up your Qi channels and that opening and movement of Qi together produce a feeling of warmth. For instance, spiritual texts commonly explain that when we feel warm in the heart from doing a good deed it is because that warmth is a sign of Qi channels opening up in the vicinity of the heart chakra. You do a good deed, your Qi moves in response, your energy channels are thereby stimulated and open a bit, and you feel warmth in your body where that happens.

You can indeed augment your Qi on the path of self-cultivation by altruistic acts of morality, namely by practicing virtuous behavior on a regular basis as Liao Fan and Franklin demonstrated. However, you can lose your Qi if you end up becoming controlled by your senses or fused to desires such as in overeating, consistently becoming drunk, engaging in substance abuse, or dropping too deeply into other sensory enjoyments such as excessive sex. This lack of moderation for sensual gratification falls into the realm of the animals.

Taoism and Chinese medicine further explain that your Qi will become damaged by external forces (environmental influences) and can be harmed when you become misled by outer things. In other words, through fascination you can become fused with external stimuli and then cling to the internal emotions or impulses that arise in response. You then "fall" by succumbing to the pursuit of the senses.

This parallels the philosophy of Yoga that human beings must not become misled by their senses. Yoga also states, as do most religions, that the spiritual path entails practicing sense control so that various desires, impulses, wishes, hungers or emotions do not pull us into incorrect acts of dissipation or wrong modes of behavior. For instance, at one time King David of the Bible lusted after the wife of Uriah the Hittite, so he sent Uriah into battle so that he would be killed by enemy soldiers, thus clearing the way for David to have sex with Uriah's wife. This is an example of being ruled by the senses.

Confucianism correctly recognizes that your will can move your Qi, which is actually the basis behind Nyasa Yoga, Tantric Yoga, Nath Yoga, Vajrayana, Taoist nei-gong and nei-dan, qi-gong and many other schools of internal Qi cultivation. You should certainly learn how to internally move your Qi as this is the way to transform your physical body and generate a strong subtle body made of Qi. To learn how to manage, guide or control the changes of phenomena – which certainly includes learning how to move your Qi to open up your Qi channels and do this – is one of the unspoken but genuine principles of Confucianism. It is something you must learn to master not only as a regular human skill but because it can produce tremendous health benefits. It is also the road for becoming a true sage.

Learning proper behavior, which means appropriate action in the world, definitely includes how to use your will to move your Qi in the right fashion. Therefore it is not only proper, but *imperative* that people who practice Confucian mindfulness also take up inner energy work in the pursuit to master this skill.

In the Confucian way that helps move society to a higher level of being, people must become masters of their bodies both internally and externally. This is a health issue and a spiritual issue, as well as a mental issue because of the tie-in between your thoughts and the smoothness of your internal Qi flow. To become a more "spiritual person" who rises above the animals, you must not only master the external control of your muscles but learn to better guide your thoughts and internal vital energy.

One can delve into various cultivation schools, such as those already mentioned, to find relevant inner Qi exercises so that you can learn how to master various internal energy cultivation techniques. This is why I wrote *Nyasa Yoga* and *Visualization Power* that contain the most powerful of these methods.

The Confucian way is to definitely take active steps to master the human body *as the function of the mind*, which is why many take up martial arts, yoga, dance or physical sports. However, the Confucian way is particularly interested in those athletic activities that can also lead to control of internal energy because this is a more important part of the spiritual path than simply exercise. Those who train the Confucian way practice using their will to control their thoughts and behavior, and also practice using their willpower to move and guide their muscles and internal energy to transform their physical body.

In recognizing the importance of both mindfulness meditation (watching thoughts) and internal Qi cultivation (which involves the process of purifying your Qi and Qi channels), we can correctly say that the Confucian way stresses mind-body cultivation with a particular emphasis on mental purity and virtuous behavior. Other spiritual schools say that our Qi and our thoughts are linked where our thoughts can move our Qi and sometimes inner Qi movements give rise to thoughts. Confucianism simply tells us that we should cultivate both our thoughts and our Qi, and that our Qi is also affected by our behavior.

Our actions (behavior) are essentially our thoughts expressed, so the basic purifying spiritual path of the world, just as is found in the Confucian way, cannot be divorced from watching your mind in order to elevate your words and behavior. You must work at self-improvement to purify your mind, learn how to deal with many types of mental activity, and purify your outward behavior too. You must learn to create your own ethical views and values, live your life in harmony with those views and values, and propagate through actions the virtuous views and values you have chosen. A life of grace is one where we can authentically express our deepest values and who we are without having to act artificially by going against them.

Thinking kind thoughts, doing good deeds, refraining from evil or errant ways, and uplifting your behavior *is* the spiritual path. This road of practice will transform your character, raising you above your lower nature. It will also transform your Qi and Qi channels so that you attain greater health and longevity. It will transform your fate, fortune and destiny as well. At its utmost peak, which is the most important thing, the mind-body path of the Confucian way will also lead to the spiritual achievement of the Tao, which is the accomplishment of becoming a sage (enlightened).

CHAPTER 8:
ACT AND OTHER METHODS FOR CHANGING HABITS AND SILENCING AFFLICTIONS

The Confucian way emphasizes that we constantly observe our minds in order to discipline our thoughts. Watching our thoughts enables us to correct and then elevate our thoughts, words and behavior. The emphasis on proper behavior towards others is how culture and civilization have appeared in the world as well as why cooperative societies have appeared where people do not solely pursue their own self-interests at the expense of others.

This is how we have divinized the human being. Culture has allowed us to trust one another and rise above the realm of the animals who are always being eaten by one another and thus doomed to constant fear. Culture, which Confucius emphasized through the promotion of standards of behavior (ritual or rites), elevates the human psyche. The pursuit of culture pacifies both the participating individual and greater society.

World cultures often tell some tale that divine beings came down from the heavens to bestow a glorious civilization upon mankind, but the truth is that our forbears developed it through virtuous actions and coordinated cooperation among people that elevated us above the cruelty of nature. We developed culture on our own by mastering self-control and promoting behavior that separated us more and more from simply being animals.

The Confucian emphasis on virtuous manners along with the practice of mindfulness for behavioral self-correction are some of the methods that help elevate and purify us. They spiritualize us by taking us above our lower natures and the unthinking behavior of animals.

To imagine what it would be like without culture and civilization, which is what the world previously experienced at various points of time, just remember all the movies you have ever seen about the breakdown of society during the aftermath of some Armageddon where people are constantly fighting each other for resources. The Confucian way not only builds culture and civilization but works to improve our lives, and its emphasis on proper behavior can guide people even through dramatic periods of societal collapse.

For instance, since politeness and civility are the foundation of all relationships and alliances, the Confucian way emphasizes that we cultivate virtuous social skills to both create and maintain a peaceful, polite society. It teaches us to benefit both ourselves and others through cooperative unity starting from the family and then extending to society and greater groups of men. Television has been used as a substitute for involvement in the community but this is the wrong way to conduct ourselves in life.

Once the famous businessman Michael Masterson described what he felt was the best way of conducting yourself in business and other areas of your life in order to produce success, peace of mind and happiness, and I think it his words perfectly encapsulate the Confucian way: "In every relationship you get into – every business, social, or personal transaction – make sure that the other person gets as much benefit from it as you do. When considering your own advantages and disadvantages in taking any course of action, consider those of everyone else involved." Another businessman started off all his negotiations with others using the admirable words, "Let's see who can benefit the other the most." This expresses the Confucian way.

The idea of individuals creating a benefit for one another is a healthy basis for the creation of a peaceful and productive society that can move forward. In fact, the ideal of Confucian propriety is that we live our lives in a way where we can actually benefit others, and thus benefit ourselves rather than become a burden on our family, friends, colleagues, strangers or society.

As previously taught, the Confucian way not only improves personal behavior and leads to better outcomes for ourselves and society, but the methods it espouses also give us the ability to personally improve our health and longevity, make spiritual progress, and improve what has been willed to us as our personal fate, fortune or destiny.

One of the closest equivalents to Confucian cultivation can be found in the powerful field of Acceptance and Commitment Therapy (ACT), which is a behavioral therapy being used by a growing number of psychologists that emphasizes living in the present moment through mindfulness. It is designed to help people bring about personal change in their lives. Its methods have many parallels to those of Confucian cultivation because its roots draw strongly from the practice of mindfulness.

As with the Confucian way, ACT states that changing our thoughts and emotions to something better requires progress through several steps. The first step is to recognize that the images, perceptions, thoughts, emotions, desires, urges and memories that arise in our mind do so naturally, automatically. They are not are fault. The mind produces thoughts ceaselessly even when we don't ask for them.

A mind (consciousness) always gives birth to thoughts. They come as they please in response to conditions and circumstances, and then they automatically disappear unless we hold onto them. Their arrival and disappearance happens quite naturally just as the knowingness of thoughts happens automatically. All the while thoughts are just objects in the mind rather than a "true reality." They are a portion of consciousness.

In other words, consciousness is always moving to spin thoughts but is itself actually just an automatic process going on within your brain – it just functions automatically - so there is no reason to berate yourself for having negative thoughts that automatically arise. Whatever arises isn't necessarily true either. Thoughts just automatically happen because you have no control over what arises within your consciousness, but you do have control over what you will do with the thoughts that appear!

When negative thoughts, afflictions or distractions appear in the mind you have to learn how to deal with them. The first thing is not to become entangled with them. They are something you must stand apart from and simply use.

Remember that since consciousness just automatically happens, it is what we do with our thoughts that counts. It is what we do with our consciousness that makes us men of consummate behavior or lowlife scoundrels akin to animals. Intentional thinking, rationality or conceptualization means creating and manipulating objects in our minds on purpose. In life we need to learn how to create useful mental thoughts so that we can do whatever we want to do. We therefore need to master the skills of intentional thinking, deliberate mental imagery and concentration to create exactly what we want in our minds. As for those thoughts that arise naturally/automatically we have to learn how to relate to them properly because we cannot stop their automatic generation. We don't have to take all our thoughts with the same degree of seriousness. What we have to learn in life is not just how to create the ones we want but how to deal with errant, unwholesome, nuisance or unflattering thoughts that afflict us because they appear, stay around and won't immediately leave.

The "Great Learning" in life therefore entails learning how to create the thoughts we need and how to manage thoughts in general. It involves mastering the mind, namely learning how to manage the mental processes of consciousness to produce the best results. As Confucius taught, the first step to this is awareness. You are to first become clearly aware of whatever is in your mind, namely your thoughts and emotions, and then make use of the beneficial thoughts that have arisen or create new ones to replace them. You should always avoid investing in thoughts that take you away from your higher values, and the detachment of mindfulness teaches you how to do this.

After they arrive, ACT says that we normally put emotional perceptions on thoughts even though whatever arises is just a bunch of neutral words, feelings and pictures that only has a meaning we give to them. Our thoughts and perceptions that arise pass through the network of our memories and become tainted by all sorts of emotional baggage including strong feelings of like and dislike. Many people may view the same thing in the world but each of us will add different emotions to the picture because the workings of our brains will automatically associate whatever we see with prior memories and emotions.

However, whatever naturally arises in the mind without effort and whatever we create on purpose are still just neutral mental events; thoughts, images or emotions are just experiences of consciousness and nothing more. They aren't a reality. You have to learn to treat them that way rather than taking them as an absolute truth. Non-judgment, or dispassionate observation of your thoughts (sometimes called "detachment") will help you quiet this internal dialogue of your mind. You can learn how to view your own thoughts dispassionately, without clinging or attachment, through the practices of meditation and mindfulness.

Concepts and emotions are just moments of consciousness without any lasting reality, and they don't necessarily reflect a truthful or accurate judgment about your circumstances either. They are a guess at what reality means. Because they appear in consciousness, however, we have to learn how to deal with them skillfully or they can cause ourselves and others a great deal of trouble, especially if they turn into errant behavior. Afflictions that continually appear in the mind, for instance, often turn into wrongdoing.

Thus, the subsequent step of the mental process is that we put emotions on the sensory perceptions or thoughts that automatically arise within our minds while forgetting that whatever arises are just neutral words and pictures. For instance, when you "hear a robin singing" all you ever actually hear, by virtue of having ears, is sound. However, to "hear a robin singing" you are actually hearing all sorts of other things besides sound such as your memories, mental habits and feelings. This additional layer we add to our thoughts and sensory perceptions is usually an evaluative judgment good just for our self alone, so this is where we get into trouble. Our emotions that we add onto things only belong to us and aren't universal reality. Too often we invest in these personal perceptions that don't hold for everyone and become too wed to them to our detriment.

The Aghora tradition of India also suggests that we stop putting emotional judgment on whatever arises in the mind because it teaches that when the mind is free of such emotional latherings it will bear no botheration for fortune and misfortune. It can make much better decisions when unhampered by personal emotions. Aghora teaches that whatever arises as our fortune in life has already happened, so there is no reason to fear it or make it worse via the negative workings of our mind. We are to accept it if it cannot be changed or change it if we can. On no account should we invest in adding more undue negative emotions to what has already happened.

We are at our best when we don't operate under the sticky influence of errant emotions lathering our thoughts. As the Confucian way teaches, we must learn to separate from thoughts and emotions to avoid mistakes in how we use the mind. We must develop an independent distance from them so that they don't automatically control our actions. We want to work to gain the skill of not being controlled by instincts, emotions, appetites and impulses but instead oncerned with higher ideals.

We never have to identify with our thoughts and emotions completely. Through awareness – the light of the mind - we should naturally recognize that they exist but we only need to employ the useful ones without investing in them as absolute realities. Instead of blindly following the urges, desires and impulses that arise in our mind, however compelling or attractive they may be, we must learn to choose behavior that embodies the highest principles of virtue and propriety we know. To elevate ourselves as spiritual beings, we need to choose noblest ways that will most separate us from a selfish, animalistic nature.

By treating thoughts as just things in the mind that we need not follow, we thereby liberate ourselves from identification with our automatically functioning lower natures and through this transcension can choose better decisions for life. Since we cannot stop thoughts from arising, this is the spiritual path of liberation because it frees us from the influence of lower thoughts and inclinations. It frees us from Nature. It involves recognizing that the world seen in consciousness is of the nature of consciousness, and those images can be dealt with skillfully when the know-how is learned.

Thoughts are just some of the objects appearing in consciousness as are images, sensations and emotions. Whatever happens to you just happens in your consciousness so the path of spirituality is all about training yourself about how to deal with your consciousness. Religion is ultimately this training and its linkage to your behavior. It is all about training, purifying, mastering, controlling or transforming consciousness … however you want to word it. It is about correctly, properly, ethically using and elevating the very thing that gives us sentience.

Spiritual liberation thus means developing a detached transcendence over thoughts so that we don't just always blindly follow the first thing that pops into our minds. In life we are to learn how to become liberated from the mind, which means to view the objects of consciousness as objects that might make us itch but which don't have to make us scratch. We must learn how to manipulate those objects and become their master. It means learning how to use consciousness correctly to help it generate what we want because the mind can and must be a tool of accomplishment and elevation. Liberation means rising above ordinary thoughts by creating higher thoughts to follow that represent the highest of human values.

Liberation involves learning how to generate the right thoughts on purpose, which we call "thinking," "discrimination," "deliberation," "intentional thinking," "wisdom," or "rationality," and properly dealing with the automatic thoughts that arise within us that we normally cannot control. Many of those can be classified as animalistic, impulsive desires and others are just afflictions or habit energies we cannot control. You can gauge the degree of someone's spirituality by examining how far their behavior differs from animals. Their behavior indicates mastery of their automatic and intentional thought processes and how much each controls their actions.

Liberation doesn't just mean being free of thoughts (being internally quiet or peaceful) or being non-attached to thoughts but also means controlling your thoughts such as having the ability to generate the thoughts you need to do what you want. Generating or choosing the right thoughts to follow is called wisdom, which requires much learning or experience, and the Great Learning in life involves cultivating wisdom as to the right types of thoughts to generate and follow, and how to do so. We don't have to be perfectly right about the world but our decisions do have to make the highest rational sense possible, and that is called pursuing wisdom in our actions. On wisdom Confucius commented, "By three methods we may learn wisdom. First, by reflection, which is noblest; Second, by imitation, which is easiest; and third by experience, which is bitterest."

When the mind isn't quiet, wisdom also involves refraining from getting caught up in the negative, afflictive or discursive thoughts and emotions arising constantly in our minds so that we only follow those that move us in higher directions. We cannot always silence wrong thoughts so as human beings we need to learn how to unhook ourselves or defuse from any negative thoughts, urges, desires or other afflictions that arise.

Both ACT and the Confucian way of mindfulness teach us how to do this. We must all gain control over the mental process that selects which thoughts to follow. We must learn to react correctly to thoughts and *follow wisdom* or skillfulness rather than whatever automatically arises in the mind, including emotional colorings, for the contents of the mind are often misleading. Spiritual cultivation is learning how to do just this.

One of the most common remedies for dealing with troublesome thoughts - which is the Confucian, Buddhist and Vedantist Way - is to develop a detached awareness of inner thoughts that is called the witness-consciousness. The witness-consciousness simply means cultivating a transcending awareness stance, like a third person observer, that is free from the pull of the thoughts that arise within consciousness. Being above, separated or detached from thoughts gives you the independence to choose wise action over just blindly following the random thoughts appearing within your brain which you should work to quell through meditation and other mental practices in the first place.

The Confucian way, like Buddhism, pragmatism and other major religions, therefore espouses that you cultivate wisdom. Wisdom means good judgment. It means good thinking which usually (but not always) produces a good result, or even superlative result. In life you need to see all your thoughts clearly without getting caught up in them, and also develop the wisest course of action for performing their objective rather than simply accepting that your present thoughts are the best way to act. If you don't know how to do something, then wisdom means you should seek out the best means possible and learn how to do it. You can develop all sorts of skills for life, but they are ultimately mental skills since thoughts control your behavior. Learning how to do something is also called the cultivation of wisdom.

Wisdom enables you to make good decisions that are not just good for you but good for others, and not just good for the present but good for the future. Wisdom teaches you how to put your virtues into practice according to the where, when and how. It enables you to discern situations clearly and basically act properly.

If you need to develop new thought directions to determine a best course of action for some challenge then you must engage in what Confucianism calls "study" or "learning." This could mean anything from analyzing the situation at hand, researching for answers or benchmarking to find the best methods or models of performance available to solve the problem. Developing new talents and skills is also a form of learning or study.

The point is to never just follow whatever pops into your mind, much of which is just plain wrong, distorted, or non-optimal because of biased emotions, wrong assumptions or simply incorrect thinking. You have to learn to improve upon what naturally arises within your brain. If you are to form habits, then form habits of the highest and best that ennoble and dignify you or which take you to peak excellence so that those reactions can become automatic.

For life you need clear thinking to determine what to do in any situation. The mind is a tool, and the great task in life is to learn how to use this tool correctly. You need to learn how to generate the thoughts you need and *ignore the thoughts you don't need*. You also need to learn how to change habit energies that might automatically impel you in negative ways.

This is the transcendence path of the Confucian way. You train to gain the capability to generate the thoughts you need through study and mastery of skills such as logic, reasoning, concentration, visualization practice and other mental skills you can cultivate. You also train to attain a degree of mental quiet and clarity – called awareness, clarity or emptiness in other cultivation schools. You train to gain the capability to rise above your automatic thoughts and habit energies, rather than just impulsively respond to them, through sitting meditation practice and Confucian mindfulness.

Mastering your mind through these (and other) practices, which enable you to gain control over both the automatic and rational thinking processes of your mind, qualify you to become a full human being, so this is the spiritual path. What did you think it was… worship? Add to this mastery of your body, its internal energy, and your outer behavior and the path description is pretty complete.

In essence you are fundamentally the Supreme Ultimate or original nature that has somehow, over eons, formed itself into you and everything else in the universe. There is no plan for you in the universe from this process, so you have to make one for yourself. You have to determine for yourself a life purpose or set of purposes in life which will make it worthwhile.

From the aspect of the Supreme Ultimate nothing else exists except It – no phenomena exist at all because everything is just the Supreme Ultimate in a different form. From the aspect of looking at things in terms of energy you are not a living being but just another energetic phenomena of the Supreme Ultimate. On a conventional level we say that you are a living being but this ultimately means nothing other than that you are one of the phenomenon in the universe with sentience or consciousness. The miracle of existence is that you have this consciousness and can think and know while other phenomena cannot. The great wondrous miracle of life is this gift of consciousness, and your mind is actually the "wish fulfilling gem" of Buddhism and Hinduism that gives you cognizance and enables you to create what you want. In life you must therefore learn to master this great miracle, this great gift that other phenomena lack.

From the practical aspect you *are* indeed a living being with consciousness (a phenomena produced within the Supreme Ultimate) and it is within your capabilities to not just remain a simple animal but to master your mind, body and behavior to reach the highest possible degrees of dignity and ennoblement, which is the status of a sage. For instance, you can even form a spiritual body that has vast capabilities and lets you live as long as the heavens. To do so you must make your mind a tool that can help you spiritualize your existence. Regardless of your status in life – whether rich or poor, high or low, suffering or living in enjoyment – this is the Great Learning.

This is the highest you can accomplish in life, which is to become master of your mind and elevate your thoughts, body, speech and behavior. The method is to transcend consciousness by centering yourself in the detached observer function that can pick and choose proper thoughts from the options that you generate within your mind. If you don't like whatever automatically appears, you simply ignore it and then generate new thoughts until you attain the high standards you want.

This means that you should always study to improve yourself just as Benjamin Franklin did. You need to master the best models of reasoning and rational decision making to generate correct concepts and make great decisions. You also need to learn how to learn to master new skills as necessary. In general, we can say that you just need to learn how to best use your consciousness, i.e. your mind. Through mastery of your mind you can learn to master thousands of functions including your behavior. You can control the movements of your physical body, its internal energy, your speech and your actions. Through these skills you can then develop the best aspects of human nature and human excellence. How is this not a spiritual path?

Once again please remember that the judgments we usually place on mental phenomena cannot be said to be "universal" or "absolute truth" because not everyone will have the same opinions about the same phenomena. That being the case, there is no way our internal views can represent absolute takes on reality. Our mental thoughts are really just relative objects in our mind and all our opinions are conditionals related to us. In one sense we can even say they are "illusions" (falsities) since they don't represent the absolute truth for any situation.

What we perceive either through the senses or mind is *not reality* but just a personal mindset. What we perceive are just events within the mind that help us function in the world but which are not necessarily true, complete, reflective of the way things really are, nor absolute. We are only ever experiencing just consciousness, and never "a reality out there." We therefore, as part of the Great Learning of life, need to learn this fact and how to use the inner life of the mind to survive and thrive so that we can do what we want even though we are just experiencing our own consciousness.

The big question then, which is part of the Great Learning of Life, is how to properly relate to thoughts? Our lives are the creation of our minds so think carefully: is it not the thoughts we purposefully generate and how we respond to thoughts that determines life? Yes, it is the content of our thoughts and how we deal with and respond to them that matters most to sentient life, for sentient life means consciousness and consciousness is thoughts. Your consciousness *is* your life experience. Furthermore, thoughts produce actions so thoughts are supreme.

Thoughts are just internal words and pictures that appear in our minds. Emotions, desires, impulses, intuition, attitudes, thinking, sights, sounds, odors, tastes, physical sensations ... they are all just thoughts in the brain. Without a mind you cannot know them or anything. They are part of an internal language of consciousness that appears in our heads, some of which just automatically happens and some of which we deliberately generate by will. Reality is *not* exactly *what they are*, and yet we usually heavily invest in them without carefully editing that content using deep reason and wisdom. The bigger problem is that we often *fuse* with incorrect thoughts and emotions to our great detriment. If we simply dealt with them as objects of the mind rather than become intractably entangled with them as realities then we could avoid untold amounts of error, pain and suffering.

One of the most highly sought after life skills is the ability to be so detached from thoughts that we attain a flexibility of mind easily able to challenge prevailing assumptions and conclusions. A great mental skill is to be able to challenge the status quo and discern truth from error regardless of biases. Like Sherlock Holmes we need to learn strict rules of logic and inference so that we do not rashly jump to conclusions in our thinking. This can be done with training. For instance, a doctor is taught to rely on sound reasoning to make his medical diagnoses just as a police detective is taught to ask "Cui Bono" ("who benefits?") to solve crimes. There are all sorts of mental skills we can and should learn like this that involve becoming less wed to emotional reactions or incorrect notions, but which treat thoughts as objects subject to the sieve of wise judgment and reason.

For instance, a true student of the Confucian way examines history to derive principles of behavior and to form models of expectations, which is why Confucius said, "Study the past if you would define the future." Along these lines, tradition can sometimes be used to solve the problems of the present. However, the exemplary man never becomes wed to traditional solutions, nor to his study of history or his models for predicting human behavior. Why? Because there is always room for error. He develops the habit of caution in reasoning to conclusions and the habit of egolessness in correcting his errors. This is how to use the mind rightly. He keeps his eye on his predictions to see how they are doing and immediately abandons his working hypotheses when evidence shows errors, correcting things as need be.

In *Analects* 2.18 Confucius also taught this principle of mental behavior, cautioning us against jumping to conclusions and relying on unproven hypotheses. When Zizhang was studying with the aim to secure the post of being an official Confucius said, "Emphasize listening and put aside what is uncertain." In other words, using the mind correctly means listening, studying or investigating to ascertain true facts, and in dealing with ambiguity you should not rely on unproven conjectures.

ACT reminds us that whenever thoughts arise in our minds we need not fuse with them, fight them, run from them or give them more undue attention than they deserve. This extends to emotions, desires, impulses, habits, inclinations, mental pictures, sound memories, sensory images and so on. It also extends to all models, algorithms, rules, principles or representations we mentally use to handle our behavior for they are also rarely sacrosanct. Who can say what behavior is right for any situation? Wisdom can only guide us as to what we may think is best, but no one knows what is best for sure. However, the training that leads to the best you can possibly offer (despite the possibility of error) is wisdom training, and that is the spiritual road.

Many things daily appear in our minds, much of which afflicts us, and the teachings of ACT are very useful for helping us deal with the barrage of negative self-talk, negative emotions and all sorts of other mental problems, such as addictions, that continually return to haunt us. In conjunction with Confucian mindfulness teachings and meditation, learning ACT can help you master your mental realm.

ACT was developed because bad thoughts or emotions often appear in our minds to afflict us without leaving, and some *consistently* afflict us. ACT helps us manage the onslaught against our mental health and wellbeing. We must learn how to invest only in valuable thoughts that will lead us forwards, but how do we handle the errant thoughts and emotions that keep popping up in our minds and create an imaginary pressure urging us to follow negative inclinations? We need to respond correctly to those pressures when they won't go away, and must never lose our ethical bearings due to their promptings. ACT helps us do this just like the Confucian way.

Addictions to alcohol or gambling and even phobias are perfect instances where we want to ignore or override those impulses yet find this extremely difficult to do. A thought/urge to drink or gamble can become like a command that addicts must obey even though they know it is destroying their lives. Some people know that a particular thought will lead to peril or destruction, yet cannot stop themselves from treating it as if it were a rule they must succumb to.

Whenever negative afflictions like this arise in our mind we can turn to the various remedies suggested by the world's spiritual schools to help us. We can try to cut them off, transform them into a higher octave, contemplate (analyze) them in order to reframe them or dissolve them at their root, engage in distractions to divert ourselves from their influences, keep distancing ourselves from them by abiding in nonattachment (detachment or separation as the observer or witness of them) until they depart, or use other various forms of skillful means to help ignore them and minimize their harmful influence.

The ACT way of dealing with things states that if you cannot leave something then you have to either (a) take action to improve it, or (b) accept it. Those are your only two choices. You can either accept what appears in your mind or take action to improve the contents of your mind.

Therefore when unwanted thoughts arise in your mind and won't leave ACT says that you either have to accept them (without necessarily acting on them) or improve the situation through some type of transformation brought about by the skillful use of your will. At the same time, the Confucian way says we must continually work for the greatest good despite whatever arises in our brain, as does Buddhism and Christianity and other spiritual schools.

ACT says that to liberate ourselves from being under the control of unwanted thoughts or emotions we must, as in the Confucian way, start by cultivating awareness. We must bring a pristine full awareness to our here-and-now situation with attention, interest and receptiveness, being open to the present experience while fully engaging with it. We must become fully aware of the contents of our mind at that time. The few things under your control in life include your attention and your actions so here we must engage our attention on what is internally mentally happening, but we should do so as a dispassionate observer just as ACT and the Confucian way recommend.

Remember that thoughts, emotions, memories, urges, attitudes and desires always arise automatically, and you have absolutely no control over whatever arises in your mind. Things just arise regardless as to what you want (unless you've undertaken lots of personal training to make certain reactions/responses automatic, such as is done in sports). Therefore you shouldn't criticize yourself for having negative thoughts and emotions. Self-criticism should only arise, if at all, in response to how you *react* to your negative thoughts. It should arise when you engage in bad behavior. If you are not working on self-improvement this absence is what must be criticized.

ACT firmly states that you should not criticize yourself for whatever automatically arises in your mind. You criticize your response. As it teaches, if you cannot leave something then you have to either take action to improve it or accept it.

You can gain control over potentially negative actions regardless of your thoughts, desires, emotions and impulses *if* you are aware of their presence *and* maintain a focus on whatever you are doing so that you ignore them and keep moving forward with perseverance. For instance, in sports the athletes are told to "feel the fear but do it anyway." During military battles soldiers conquer fear by continuing to move forward too. In stock market trading you are taught to override your screaming emotions to follow your profitable trading models. In each of these cases you maintain control over your actions by ignoring your emotions.

It takes training but you can learn how to control your actions to do what is *deemed best* despite thoughts or emotions impelling you to do otherwise. This is why Confucius is so revered, for he taught us to do exactly this. Detaching from thoughts so as to become independent enough to pick the right ones to follow, or simply overriding the bad ones, is the basis of many other eastern spiritual traditions too.

Confucian cultivation requires that you always inspect your own mind to clearly know your good and bad thoughts so that you might choose the best to follow, but sometimes personal introspection is not enough for wise decisions. Sometimes we need to seek the advice of family and friends, or even a Mastermind group that shares our interests or concerns to make wise decisions. Their opinions can serve as an independent mirror of reflexive judgment on our actions.

In Chinese culture it was considered the duty of the junior member of a hierarchy to correct the senior if the latter strayed from the ideal of proper conduct. This same idea of correcting elders who strayed held in ancient Greece as well. For instance, part of the famous Athenian Oath contained the words, "We will revere and obey the City's laws, and will do our best to incite a like reverence and respect in those above us who are prone to annul them or set them at naught."

Regardless of the heights of our position or power in society, when we cannot correct ourselves due to a lack of reflective review we need others to help us see our errant behavior so that we can correct it. The higher we climb the easier it is to become corrupted or blind hence the more we need feedback systems in order to temper incorrect behavior.

As an example, the famous Emperor of the Tang dynasty, Tang Taizong, is often argued to be the greatest leader in Chinese history because he instituted a self-corrective method related to mindfulness and self-reflection that depended upon the assistance of others. He knew that to become a great ruler he had to overcome his weaknesses such as controlling his emotions and desires, and therefore he pursued self-knowledge and self-regulation by inviting the comments and criticism of his officials.

Knowing that power tends to blind men, Tang Taizong made it a rule to ask for honest comments from his officials about his policies and behavior. He used this as a mirror to obtain the self-knowledge required for self-correction when he had blinded himself from reality. George Marshall, one of America's most revered military figures who was known for his personal virtues, also prized frank appraisal of his actions/policies and criticized his men for not providing it to him. Self-knowledge, which you can attain in various ways, is what these men of power were searching for.

Self-knowledge leads to self-change, personality-change leads to behavioral changes, and those changes should improve matters for everyone. That's the goal in life for personal cultivation and Confucianism. As to the larger picture involving organizations, as previously discussed even a modern government needs a free press that reports on its activities because the honest reporting will serve as a mirror of self-knowledge. A clear reporting is necessary to minimize government corruption and hold the government accountable to the public good.

This is also the Confucian way. The Confucian way means self-correction, correcting phenomena and correcting society. Each has to become better. It means correcting people, families, communities, societies, organizations and even the government, just as Confucius taught. The Confucian way is that you train not only your thoughts to the best degree possible, but also become master of yourself and "the changes" to the extent that you become able to improve society. The ultimate purpose of self-training is an active social position in the world that has a beneficial impact on society and the greater good.

As Confucius said, this all starts with awareness. Awareness means self-observation, which leads to the breaking of attachments – mental attachments and habits. Mindfulness practice leads to the breaking of mental attachments as well because that third-person separation provides a degree of freedom or liberation from the workings of the mind including automatic thoughts whose arising cannot be thwarted. For those mental functions that can be controlled, the Confucian way also involves the discipline of self-correction once you have some awareness of what is wrong either mentally or behaviorally.

The Confucian way basically involves two drives toward mental perfection: (a) effectively dealing with the automatic processes of the mind, some of which produce mental afflictions that won't leave or are temporary distractions that interrupt concentration, and (b) developing *to the utmost* the many countless rational and creative functions of the mind including thinking and reasoning, concentration and attentiveness, visualization and imagination, control of the body and its vital Qi energy, control of speech and actions (behavior), the pursuit of virtue, transcendence over our animal nature, and so on. With this understanding, self-perfection then involves a pursuit to master (1) automatic and (2) deliberate or intentional mental processes of consciousness.

When awareness is mastered the skill of focus becomes possible and with concentration skills you can go on to develop even more mental skills. Mastering mindful awareness gives you the ability to focus your mind with attentive interest for a long period of time and stay concentrated rather than succumb to distraction. As part of the Great Learning in life you need to train your mind so that your attention can stay with your thoughts and intentions (behaviors, commitments, projects, etc.) that are proper and useful despite distractions that might pull you in other directions.

Training to develop concentration enables you to persevere with grit, tenacity and doggedness on any path of your choosing even though you might experience challenges, difficulty, deprivation and failure. Concentration and perseverance train you to be able to set aside current gratification for longer-term goals – one of the key attributes of those who are successful in life. It enables you to continually maintain a hold on correct principles of thinking and behavior rather than succumb to the irrational mind, animal instincts, or errant emotions.

Life requires that we achieve mastery in the skills necessary for survival and self-interest. This includes problem solving, critical thinking and countless skills of the mind such as organizational skills or abilities such as mathematics or a good memory and so on. What you want to pursue to develop as a skill is up to you. However, all of these possibilities require a degree of self-knowledge, self-confidence, concentration, perseverance and a personal premium placed on self-mastery and self-education.

Heroes are born from Confucian cultivation not because they follow the road of conformity, but because they develop such skills and put them to use for the self and others. They learn how to manage their mind and its ability to manipulate their body, its energy, and their behavior. They develop strong positive character traits by following a road of personal development, each person emphasizing different things they want to master, and then blaze new trails for society. They learn to think for themselves independently rather than blindly submit to the conclusions of social groupthink. Because they learn to think for themselves they typically develop a strong personal moral value system. Like Sikhs they usually stick up for what is right in the name of righteousness and follow their own values when higher than those of society. For instance, Confucius married his own daughter to a man who had spent some time in jail, but not because of any guilt on his part. A typical Chinese father of his time would never have arranged such a union, but Confucius did what he thought was right despite the views of society. Can you be so strong yourself?

How can we become strong enough as individuals to actually go against the notions of society when we think them wrong? By strengthening our own internal moral compass, for that is part of the Great Learning. When you think things through thoroughly enough to develop your own independent convictions, that is evidence of the proper Confucian way.

Vedanta teaches that there is always a part of us, like a third person observer, which is outside the stream of thoughts running within our mind. This formless observer seems outside of the contents of consciousness because it knows them. There is a part of us that can observe difficult thoughts and feelings without being hurt by them because it transcends them, and therefore does not have to act on them. ACT simply says that we can recognize that "they are not a threat to me," which enables us to deal with difficult thoughts and choose the right ones to follow. Being clear and unbiased by cultivating a separation from thoughts and emotions, we can thereby form better ideas and select the ones that are correct to act upon.

This transcendental observer part of consciousness is ever-present and impervious to harm no matter what thoughts, emotions, sensations, or other mental objects arise within the mind of consciousness. Our ability for self-observation is sometimes referred to in various spiritual schools as a pure awareness that has no physical properties, but that is only a way of talking since awareness is always caught up with an I-center within consciousness. It, too, is not actually transcendental but just a thought product created by the functioning of the mind. Without that I-thought or I-center there is no way to know (be aware of) anything, and thus calling it a transcendent part of us and so forth are only ways of talking. Nevertheless, this way of talking can help us detach from thoughts and cultivate greater mental freedom.

The Buddhist way, like ACT, says that this formless observer is what we must cultivate in life because it is the key to all our higher mental skills, such as our rational intentional thinking. Its existence gives us a power of mental detachment, and from detachment is derived the power to select the proper thoughts to act upon or the power to recognize that we need to generate new thoughts to handle a situation better. Being detached from thoughts but knowing them allows us to dispassionately watch our thoughts. It allows us to separate from them and treat them as objects to be manipulated rather than commands we must follow, as sometimes happens when emotions overwhelm us and take control of our mind.

For the Confucian way and ACT, you must become fully engaged in whatever you are doing, fully present with attention concerning whatever you are dealing with. If unhelpful thoughts or emotions arise, ACT teaches that you should try to defuse from them such as by saying to yourself, "I'm having the thought that [etcetera]" or "I notice that I'm having the thought that [etcetera]." This helps you create a distance from the thoughts and emotions by labeling them as simply a mental experience, which is exactly what they are.

This distancing is extremely powerful because it helps prevent you from becoming so entangled in mental experiences that you lose an independent perspective and automatically follow lower animalistic or emotional leanings. Unchecked emotions, especially, can silence logic and rational thinking to lead you down harmful paths.

When unpleasant feelings or emotions arise in your mind, such as anxiety or fear, the positive way of dealing with them is by not fusing with them. You need to acknowledge that they are there but should train your mental processes so that you do not become entwined with them. Otherwise you will be turning them over and over again in your head bathing in afflictions.

Those who practice meditation and mindfulness have an edge over others because they gradually attain this ability of detached independence over thinking. They learn to stay centered in the transcendent, observer part of consciousness which recognizes that thoughts are just mental objects. Being partially freed from the pressure they normally bear upon us it becomes easier for them not to react to unwholesome thoughts and emotions.

There are many methods of dealing with troublesome or bothersome thoughts and emotions that continually, habitually arise to afflict you. Suppressing them is impossible to do completely since the mind operates automatically and such thoughts will always sprout when they want. We therefore need methods to deal with their eruptions.

The most common remedy is to master detachment from the contents of the mind, which makes them easier to handle. Through detachment we can simply choose to act only on those thoughts that represent our values. However, if they continue to afflict us then we will still need some way to reduce their reoccurrences and pressure.

In both ACT and the Confucian way you must pay careful attention to whatever you are doing and to the effects you are having so that you can always correct/edit your thoughts, actions and behavior. The measuring stick of your progress is the purity or impurity of the thoughts you tend to deal with, your inner calmness, serenity or peace of mind, and the virtuousness as well as effectiveness of your outer behavior.

In life you actually have no control over what thoughts will arise within you just as you have no control over what circumstances will arise to greet you. There may come times when you feel desperate, needy or tortured by reality and everything is awful but you still have to mentally deal with this. The Confucian way trains you on what to do.

Right now you actually have no control over other people or the world around you, or even whether you will be alive tomorrow. You also have no control over whether your actions will bear the fruit you want. Let's be honest and also admit that life is often crap - it doesn't always bring us what we want and you often have to "put up with shit" just to make a living. That being the case, you have to figure out how to get what you want or how to change situations for the better. You need to figure out what really matters in life as well as how you should think and behave in good times and bad times, especially when you land in unfortunate circumstances you cannot escape.

Your actions socially interact with people and the world around you and can affect them, but your actions are really the only thing under your control rather than the results you want to bring about. You only have control over your actions in life, but no control over the results of your actions. Whether you are experiencing good or bad fortune the only thing you can ever control are your actions and the commitment to following the right way to behave. Everything in life is impermanent but within that stream of impermanence you can hold fast to an ideal of greatness – that of cultivating virtuous responses regardless of whatever happens.

When you must take action to solve some problem or address some situation, the Confucian way is take actions guided by your highest values to solve them. Here is the measure of the human being … can you persevere with actions in line with your values despite temptations to drop them? Can you always do what is right in the face of extreme difficulty? Can you live in a proper way that you actually benefit others without becoming a burden?

Your future is not under your absolute control, whereas what is under your control is your ability to perform actions with value even in the midst of misfortune urging you otherwise. All you can do in life is keep moving forward in a direction that you value that in itself embodies the highest principles of humanity. This is one of the mainstays of non-denominational spiritual ethics.

The Confucian way is that in whatever you do, whether you are experiencing tremendously good or horrifically bad fortune, you are to always remain faithful to your personal values that must be of the highest ethics. Actions are your will expressed that demonstrate your values. Of course you can never be "perfectly good" in any situation but you can always *lean towards being as good as you can be*. You can always lean towards cooperative help and away from simply satisfying your own desires. This is what makes you fully human rather than an animal.

Actually, adopting this one principle alone of "leaning towards the good as much as possible" sets you apart from most humans and spiritualizes you to some extent. Few religious teachings are higher than this. In a sense it is similar to "Do unto others as you would have them do unto you" or Jesus's dictum to love your neighbor as thyself.

This is the Great Learning in life, namely how to select a valuable journey and persevere in that goal while acting in accordance with the highest ethics and values to get there – always maximally leaning towards the good. There will certainly be obstacles along the way but you are to greet these challenges with the highest values possible.

Once again, you should never meld or fuse with the negative contents of consciousness that arise along this journey. You should acknowledge them for what they are and keep moving forward despite any mental sufferings and afflictions. Remember that for adversity to transform into suffering your mind has to get into action. Mindfulness can help prevent you from letting your mental realm transform form into that scenario of suffering.

You always have a choice on how much attention to pay to your negative thoughts. For instance, there are many ways to handle negative internal dialogue and afflictions but the most important thing is to be present in accepting your thoughts and feelings, overriding them whenever errant so that you connect with your highest values, and taking effective action despite any interference they may provide.

The practice of meditation and mindfulness inherent to ACT and the Confucian way reduce mental distractions, mental afflictions and your internal dialogue over time. These two practices teach you to sustain your attention (concentration) even in the midst of distractions such as negative self-talk. Mindfulness leads to an improved ability to focus on performance and the ability to accomplish any goals you seek in life. With mindfulness your attention becomes automatic.

On the other hand, when mindfulness is not enough to keep you on track because negative thoughts and afflictions become too strong, you need to learn another mental skill, namely how to intentionally shift to more positive thoughts and feelings that don't defile your mental state. Luckily there are many strategies that can assist people to do this when they are still on the learning curve in their application of ACT or the Confucian way. When people need more help with handling mental afflictions than what meditation practice and mindfulness can provide they can turn to other techniques to help them calm their minds.

When not eliminated mental afflictions can make a hell out of heaven, and often turn into wrongdoings that produce a terrible fate or simply go against your values. Because of their unsettling nature and danger, all sorts of helpful methods have been invented to help deal with afflictions when they become too strong. Here are a few of these methods that you might want to use when afflictions reach that threshold because meditation and mindfulness are not enough.

Distraction and Avoidance

As stated, one way to handle disturbing afflictions such as overpowering emotions is through distraction. The strategy is to ignore "bad thoughts" by occupying yourself with other activities until the afflictive impulses go away. For instance, you might avoid steeping yourself in anger, sadness or depression by working out at the gym or watching TV to distract yourself from the strong emotion. As another example, men typically refrain from the urge to masturbate by occupying themselves with other activities until bedtime so that the impulsive urge disappears when they go to sleep.

Incidentally, the "Just say no" campaign to help teenagers walk away from sex assumes that they can turn passion off at will when the truth is that many teenagers cannot cope with their emotions. The better strategy for helping them stay chaste is to teach them to walk away from the first fires of passion before they get drawn in. By avoiding the problem entirely rather than dipping their toe in the water they can solve the problem through avoidance.

Wisdom teaches that you shouldn't put yourself in a position to start bad habits or succumb to your baser instincts but should avoid the potential problem and its environment in the first place. The right conduct in relation to oneself is to avoid creating bad habits that might afflict you. If you avoid creating a new harmful habit by avoiding exposure to it – such as smoking, drinking, gambling, roughnecking or drugs – then you avoid the need for a cure.

Another method to distract yourself away from disturbing emotions and mental annoyances is to occupy yourself with a hobby requiring concentration. Hobbies usually entail a strong interest to concentrate on something that can occupy your mind for hours and are another means to kill mental afflictions.

Reciting mantras, prayers, affirmations or using positive self-talk can also occupy your thoughts enough that you can put aside bad emotions or other negative inclinations when they attempt to take over your mind. They can also keep you mentally busy enough so that you do not engage in afflictive mental indulgences.

There are all sorts of other ways to practice distraction, but the basic principle is to occupy yourself with something interesting that requires concentration - other than the demanding affliction - that you can effectively ignore whatever is accosting you.

Higher Alternatives

We can also deal with afflictive thoughts and errant impulses by trying to transform them into higher alternatives. An example would be satisfying the desire to drink sugary soda pop by drinking sparkling water instead. In this way you might be placated by the bubbles rather than the sugar, and in that way can kill off the desire to drink something harmful to your health.

Another example of this technique is to take the impulse of sexual desire and re-channel that pressing urge into exercise. Some individuals dissipate it through strenuous *kumbhaka* pranayama practice (a yogic practice of holding the breath) or physical competitive sports.

To stop smoking some people substitute a less harmful habit such as wearing a nicotine patch, and from these examples you can see how you might try to re-channel thoughts or habits in a different fashion until a pressing mental affliction leaves you.

Buddhist Methods

Buddhism also has specific exercises for transforming afflictive emotions that tend to accost our minds to produce errant tendencies of behavior. It espouses specific meditation methods for turning greed into generosity, anger into patience, stupidity into wisdom, conceit into humility, and distraction into concentration. Buddhism teaches that if you don't specifically transform six root afflictions that attack everyone then ten thousand other afflictions will always be ready to sprout from these roots.

Visualization practice is another mental programming tool you can learn to help deal with bothersome thoughts/emotions. It can especially help with anxiety or fear. As detailed in my books *Visualization Power* and *Sport Visualization for the Elite Athlete*, by repeatedly mentally visualizing yourself performing a new type of perfected behavior the effort will form new neural pathways in your brain for that desired behavior. This can reduce fear as well as increase competence. Sports enthusiasts have found that the more you reinforce those neural pathways the more you will be able to draw upon those patterns at will to defeat afflictions.

Due to neural plasticity, you can use visualization practices to create new neural pathways in the brain that correspond to almost any characteristic. This includes behaviors such as generosity, courage, truthfulness and so forth. Visualization practice can be used as a type of mental programming to help replace negative afflictions, impulses, burdens, vices or "sins" with more positive counterparts you personally select as the higher way you want to act in life. If you want to become a better you, visualization practice can help you do so.

Every time your behavior follows the same mental pathway, including those forged through visualization practice, that specific pattern gets closer to becoming the pattern of automatic unconscious default. Thus, through the daily practice of visualization exercises for behaviors you want to instill in yourself (like Franklin, Liao Fan, etc.), you can actually build new behavioral patterns that can eliminate recurring mental afflictions.

Many neurolinguistic programming (NLP) practices, such as the "Circle of Excellence" technique, also train you to create positive internal states that you can call upon at will in order to deal with mental afflictions when they arise. These techniques, like visualization practice, also help you to rewire your brain and reframe emotions so that they no longer take control of your psyche.

Detoxification and Exercise

Another method of dealing with mental afflictions is to decrease their tendency to arise in the first place. This can sometimes be done by making your body more healthy when these afflictions are connected with your physiology. You make your body more healthy by exercising your muscles, rotating your internal energy everywhere, altering your diet towards more natural foods, taking supplements, and then detoxifying and supporting your body with alternative medicines (see *Detox Cleanse Your Body Quickly and Completely*). This will often reduce the volume of afflictions that arise because most thoughts are connected with your physiology, such as tending to get angry too easily when you have a weak or damaged liver or suffering from depression or mental illness due to a niacin and other B-vitamin deficiencies. By strengthening your body and its organs you can therefore reduce or eliminate certain types of recurrent mental afflictions.

Here is why this works. Your Qi and your consciousness (your thoughts, emotions, impulses and afflictions) are linked. In other words, the vital energy of your body and your thoughts are intertwined. The health of your Qi and Qi circulation throughout your body is related to your body and consciousness - your mental activity. This is a principle consistently taught by many different spiritual schools.

Pure Qi and smooth Qi circulations within your body produce a pure mind, but erratic or irregular Qi flows within you tend to cause more scattered thoughts (the "monkey mind") and improper behavioral impulses. When your Qi flow becomes smooth then the thoughts that arise in your mind will tend to become more easy and peaceful. To therefore reduce the physiological influence of your body on your mind you must work to open up your body's Qi channels everywhere. This means the pathways that penetrate every cell and tissue that you can help open by using stretching exercises, pranayama, and other detoxification techniques. Since poor Qi flow is often caused by states of illness or body imbalances, becoming healthier in all ways, especially through better nutrition and exercise that stretches all the muscles of your body (and thus all its Qi channels), will help you reduce the volume of bothersome thoughts.

Chiropractic adjustments, to help correct spinal misalignments of your nervous system are also helpful in this regard. Bodywork sessions involving deep tissue massage therapy (Rolfing, Hellerwork, etc.) and exercises such as Pilates or Yoga can help you open up your Qi channels too.

Detoxifying your body to discharge accumulated toxins and poisons, so that it reaches a higher stage of structural, biochemical and energetic balance, is also something that can greatly help because it causes you to get rid of poisons that interfere with internal Qi flow.

Remember that meditation and pranayama can help you to open up your Qi channels so that you experience a higher degree of mental peace, purity and serenity free of recurring mental afflictions. Detoxing the body in conjunction with these practices will help because they will all cleanse the energy flow lines within your cells and tissues that your vital energy has trouble traveling through.

Since the inner Qi flow of your body is intertwined with the development of your thoughts and inclinations, opening the Qi flow pathways and improving your Qi circulation will help quiet your mind and reduce mental afflictions.

Homeopathy, Acupuncture, and Other Types of Energy Work

As stated, sometimes recurring negative thoughts and emotions can be due to errant circulatory Qi flows within your body, and often these errant Qi flows can be adjusted to normal through consistent application of various forms of energy medicine.

The energy medicine modalities you might try to help heal medical conditions or reduce emotional issues include acupuncture, EFT (Emotional Freedom Technique), homeopathy and nutripuncture. Such therapies, because they are based on transforming the energies or energy pathways connected with thoughts, may help you change your thought patterns and habits of behavior.

Perfuming Permeation

Yet another method for transforming excessively negative internal dialogue is by avoiding exposure to negative influences that might kick it off and instead visiting or surrounding yourself with positive influences that will permeate your consciousness. Over time an exposure to positive environmental influences will slowly change the underlying seeds of your thoughts and behavior.

We all have innate seeds of virtuous behavior, but those moral sprouts require a proper environment and nurturing to develop as they should. The development of virtuous tendencies needs both proper instruction and a proper environment.

Continually exposing yourself to positive influences will help sprout the seeds of virtue and slowly transform your thoughts and behavior for the better, and thereby help to quell various negative mental patterns. The practice of habitually associating with positive influences will transform you in a positive way while the habit of associating with negative influences can be a road of destruction.

History states that the mother of Mencius sought the influence of a good neighborhood for her son, changing her residence three times on account of the bad influences he was encountering in the neighborhood. She changed houses each time she felt that the local environment would influence him in a negative fashion.

In moving her home, Mencius's mother showed that she knew the power that perfuming influences held for sowing the seeds of character and behavior. If a child continually associates with a negative environment they will probably absorb those tendencies, and so would you. However, associating with positive environmental influences over time will, through slow perfuming, improve your mindset and behavior. People acquire mindsets, viewpoints, virtues and skills as a result of their environments and the daily practices that they continually pursue over time, so use this to your advantage.

Reading Books

Reading the right type of books can also help you to learn how to control your thoughts, reduce afflictions, develop mental skills, change your personality, improve your character and elevate your behavior. Therefore this is another road available for helping you deal with negative thoughts and afflictions that often bother you, and is also a road for cultivating virtue.

Excellent moral examples of individuals from antiquity, both good and bad, can be found in Plutarch's *Lives of the Noble Greeks and Romans*. The beauty of Plutarch's *Lives* is that it focuses on the characters of individuals and their fortunes and misfortunes. It prompts you to think about what type of person we should become whereas modern ethics simply focuses on the right or wrong of actions. Nan Huai Chin's *Analects* also offers one of the finest explanations of Confucius's teachings on morality.

Methods for transforming your behavior so that you can cultivate a character of excellence can be found in *Liao Fan's Four Lessons*, *The Autobiography of Benjamin Franklin*, and Frank Bettger's *How I Raised Myself from Failure to Success in Selling*. Both *Move Forward* along with *Quick, Fast, Done* also join this list

For the development of mental and physical skills and how to use the mind correctly, which is also the Confucian way, there is *Visualization Power* by Bill Bodri, *The Happiness Trap* by Russ Harris, *The Power of Habit* by Charles Duhigg, and *As a Man Thinketh* by James Allen which teaches that the way you think is how the world tends to manifest. Related to these books is *Courage Under Fire* by James Bond Stockdale.

Various books that teach how to cultivate the active virtues include Dale Carnegie's *How to Win Friends and Influence People*, Napoleon Hill's *Think and Grow Rich* and *The Wisdom of Andrew Carnegie as Told to Napoleon Hill*.

For further teachings on the wisdom of living there is *The Autobiography of Benjamin Franklin* and Franklin's *The Way to Wealth*, *The Art of Worldly Wisdom* by Baltasar Gracian, *Influence* by Robert Cialdini. *Letters from a Self-Made Merchant to His Son* by George Horace Lorimer, and *Xenophan's Cyrus the Great* by Larry Hedrick.

Skill development, which includes the task of mastering virtue, is entirely a practice-based result whose deliberate, deep practice methodology can be found within *Talent is Overrated* by Geoff Colvin, *The Talent Code* by Daniel Coyle, and *The Little Book of Talent* by Daniel Coyle. These books teach how the superlative performance of excellence is not due to talent but is produced by the aggregate of countless small habits, trained to be done consistently and correctly, fitted together into one synchronized whole.

Instituting Self-Discipline by Conforming to a Higher Code of Ethics

By simply according with the proper rules of societal conduct (which Confucius referred to as rites) you can often stifle the eruption of mental afflictions through that discipline. Confucianism offers social guidelines of propriety as do other major religions such as Christianity, Hinduism, Judaism, Islam and Buddhism with its eight-fold path (right view, right thinking; right speech; right action, right living; right effort; right memory; right meditation). For instance, Moslems do not drink alcohol according to religious rules and thereby avoid the problem of alcohol addiction and drunkenness.

Some cultures so occupy you with community activities for the benefit of others that your mental concerns are trained to focus on altruism and compassion, and through this path of showing concern for others you will also be able to put aside some afflictions.

Following an ethical code of conduct will discipline your urges and elevate your life so as to take you away from many afflictive thoughts, baser impulses and negative seeds of behavior. These negative influences might still appear but will find no avenue of expression if you desire yourself to a loftier discipline. By channeling your thoughts, speech and behavior through higher cultural pathways you can keep them occupied and deny your mind and behavior an outlet for wrongdoing.

Rules of conduct and moral principles of behavior promote harmony in social interactions because they channel how society acts. Following the proper rules of conduct reduces behavioral problems so that a society runs well. They help us become morally better people. Such rules help harmonize human relations so that cooperation and friendship grows within a society, and this reduces afflictions.

Conforming to the rules of society while following the path of mindfulness of your behavior can therefore help you avoid bad outcomes and elevate your mind/behavior over time. However, one should not let such behavioral rules ossify into strict rules of conduct never to be broken. As Jesus demonstrated with the tale of pulling a donkey from a ditch on the

Sabbath, any rules are simply guidelines but not absolutes. Confucius gave several teachings that emphasized this same point. Traditional rules of behavior can and should be abandoned in special circumstances such as emergencies.

Using Contemplation to Dissolve the Root of Your Afflictions or Eliminate Being Controlled by Emotions

One of the most powerful strategies for dissolving afflictions and reducing their appearance is to ponder their past appearance with both disapproval and a remorseful heart. The focus of regret on the harm and wrongdoings they may have caused will help dissolve those afflictions and change your behavior.

The more often you examine a negative affliction and then mentally give rise to feelings of remorse and repentance for those inclinations, the more that this type of analysis will serve as a type of antidote. Contemplation on a negative impulse will change how you think about the motivations at hand and may help you turn your back on such afflictions.

This practice of analyzing your behavioral impulses is called "wisdom analysis" or the "fire of contemplation." Contemplating an affliction like this is the basis of Confucian self-reflection and many other spiritual paths. This practice of contemplation will help to unravel the hold that any non-virtuous tendency has upon your mind. You gradually work at eliminating negative tendencies by analyzing why they are improper, what harm they might cause or have caused, why they keep arising and what in general to do about them.

As Meher Baba states, contemplation is thus another way, other than mindfulness where you simply observe your thoughts, to help consume those tendencies. Contemplation, or introspective reflection where you analyze something, helps to slowly cut off afflictive mental knots and compulsions.

The use of reason in real time to deal with irrational emotions also falls into this category of using contemplation to help dissolve afflictions. Our reason is our highest nature, and it allows us to set errant emotions and baser thoughts or inclinations aside so that we are free of lower influences. We normally train to do this through mindfulness and meditation, but sometimes using reasoning, or wisdom, to work through afflictive emotions is what can free us of their influence.

We can cannot control their arousal but we can control our minds to prevent emotions from taking possession of us and causing us to act. We can also use reason to sometimes overrule passions when they overtake us. Furthermore, we can learn how to live undisturbed by our emotions rather than lose control whenever they strongly appear. A moral life *requires* a rational control of our emotions so this is something we must master in life as part of the Confucian way.

Reason (wisdom or thinking) gives us the chance to control our internal lives and the choice of whether to succumb to desires, urges, emotions, and impulses or not. It gives us the ability to control our actions, but of course this doesn't mean they can accomplish what we want. Therefore we must accept the results our actions produce in the external world, and "mastering the changes" means that we must keep working at changing those results until we finally produce/get what we want. We cannot control what the world will do, but we can control our reactions to what happens and keep working to change things until they become the way we want them to be.

Dissolving Habit Energies

Many people want to quit various negative habits such as smoking, drinking alcohol or even criticizing people but find it extremely difficult … even if they practice meditation and mindfulness. However, once you sincerely decide to start changing in a certain way then those changes can be made to become real. When we wish to modify a child's behavior we can give him direct moral instructions along with positive alternatives to the behavior we want to correct, and this helps. However, as adults who are trying to break habits to change ourselves the process is not as simple.

The Confucian way is that you must learn how to master transformations, but you need a model or guide for going about this in the most efficient manner so that you can give yourself the highest probability of success. When mindfulness and detachment or other techniques don't help, here is one of the most successful methods for breaking a habit "by transformation."

All habits are routines performed in response to a cue to obtain a reward. The key to changing habits is to first achieve a self-awareness about the rules of your habit, namely the cue and rewards that produce your habit pattern. From self-observation you can derive a full picture of your habit, and by then taking some of the power out of that pattern the habit will become easier to transform. The way to go about eliminating or transforming a habit is to first identify the full habit cycle and then experiment with various ways to interrupt it to break its hold. This includes trying to transform it into something higher.

There is no one perfect prescription for changing habits. However, there is a common scientific framework that has been found useful for understanding them so that you can more readily overcome them. Think of the problem of unwanted habits in this way. Essentially, some cue causes you to engage in a habitual routine for a specific reward that you mentally or emotionally crave. A habit means that your brain has established a formula it *automatically* follows where it sees a *cue*, and then you perform some *routine* in order to get some specific *reward*. To change this, you first have to determine the components of that circuit.

The key to breaking a habit is to use awareness to analyze what is occurring during the habit and then intervene to break the automated cycle. Thus the first two things to determine are (a) the reward you hope to receive from the habit and (b) the actual habit routine you engage in.

It takes some work to figure out the "reward" because some people don't know what they are actually seeking from their habit. Nevertheless there is always a reward being expected for the behavior otherwise the brain would not consider this particular loop worth remembering to make a habit out of it. To find the *reward* you are seeking you must test different hypotheses to determine what craving is actually the real one driving your routine. What is seeking to be satisfied? As to the *routine*, it is easy to identify because *the routine is your habit* (which can be something physical, mental or emotional) and you already know what it is.

Once you have discovered the habit loop of a routine and its satisfied craving then you can look for ways to transform that particular habit into a newer routine with better outcomes. To get rid of a habit you have the two options of either (1) dropping it entirely or (2) redesigning it into something better.

The final piece of the puzzle is determining what *triggers* the initiation of your habit energies, namely the cue. There are five cue categories that typically set off habits: location, time, emotional state, other people, or an immediately preceding action. To determine which cue triggers your habit, for several days you need to go through this list and write down these five things the very moment the habit urge hits you. From a compilation of this history you must derive an inventory of your actual triggers and then determine the most probable candidate for the cue that sets you off.

Once you know your trigger cue, your routine and your expected reward you can then work to turn off automation and become fully alive again. You can start to fiddle with these three components to re-engineer your automatic mental processes with substitutes. The goal is that with active awareness you can make behavioral choices that substitute new behaviors for old habits. That's how you break automatic habit energies.

All this requires repeated experiments to determine portions of the habit loop that might collapse it entirely. However, once you gain some self-knowledge of your trigger cues, habit routine and expected reward then you will have some power over this loop because you can try out various ways of re-engineering it. You might intervene to destroy it or create an entirely new habit to transcend it.

No specific set of steps works for everyone, but in general the best course of action for changing a habit is to keep the cue and reward, but *replace the routine with something better.* You must try alternative routines and competing habit responses whenever your trigger cue arises to see what brings satisfaction. If you can change the routine then you can shift your habit, and in this way almost any habitual behavior can be transformed.

In other words, if you use the same cue and keep the same reward you can shift the habit routine and then change your habit. For instance, when thirsty and you need a pickup, instead of drinking soda try drinking sparking water instead to see if it satisfies you. Trying different drinks instead of soda is changing the routine while keeping the reward of a pick-me-up to satisfy thirst. This type of approach of changing the routine is important when mindfulness and willpower don't seem to be enough.

We are dependent upon habits in order to live and use them every day. A habit simply means that the brain has stopped fully participating in decision-making to go automatic. Some of our habits are even harmful, but you can regain control of yourself and transcend their power by altering the routine set off by a cue that prompts you to seek a reward.

The ability to transform a habit, such as a personality trait, is one of the goals of Confucian cultivation, and another is that we learn how to build positive, virtuous habits out of choice. Typically the Confucian way is used to help us unlearn or reroute the habits we don't want. However, humans need to create habits they want to become part of their automatic behavior for specific purposes, as is done in sports training. "Mastering the changes" like this is also part of the Confucian way.

Inner Watching

The Confucian Liao Fan was taught to watch his inner thoughts and outer deeds to determine whether they were positive or negative, good or bad, high or low, helpful or non-helpful. He was taught to perform good deeds and virtuous acts instead of wrongdoings, which the Confucian way calls practicing consummate conduct or benevolence, but he needed some method to help himself continually exert himself in this direction. As Confucius said, you need to observe the standards of conduct unswervingly without going off course.

Liao Fan, as taught, therefore started recording his mindfulness efforts in a daily journal to help track his efforts and keep himself on course. By recording the plusses and minuses he achieved in trying to transform himself he developed a monitoring system that helped him change his behavior over time. Confucius would have approved of this system heartily.

In *Analects* 5.27 Confucius said, "I am exasperated! I have not yet met the person who, when faced with his own errors, takes himself to task and looks deeply at his conduct." This method helps you do just that. Confucius felt that consummate conduct (often translated as benevolence or humanity) was the center of all his teachings, and constant self-reflection was the way to achieve it. Liao Fan and Franklin showed how to institute such principles.

The great businessman and philanthropist Andrew Carnegie once recommended that everyone should construct a check chart and make a daily habit of rating themselves on each one of the following negative and positive emotions: fear, jealousy, hatred, envy, revenge, malice, greed, superstition, distrust, anger as well as love, sex, hope, faith, desire, optimism, loyalty. In *The Wisdom of Andrew Carnegie as Told to Napoleon Hill* he said, "This experiment will surprise anyone who attempts it. It may also lead to changes in one's personality which will agreeably surprise all of his associates. This is a positive approach to self-mastery."[6] Is this not similar to Liao Fan's method as well as what Confucius wanted?

If you really want to purify your mind and behavior to engage in self-transformation you should emulate the methods in *Move Forward: Powerful Strategies for Creating Better Outcomes in Life* and *Quick, Fast, Done* as closely as possible. During the day you should watch your thoughts and behavior to keep track of any violations against what is right and proper. You must learn to transcend negative thoughts and impulses by continually witnessing your mind but you shouldn't act on errant impulses, in effect distancing yourself from your thoughts so that they don't control your actions. The more you can do this the more you can cultivate your Qi channels and purify your behavior.

If you set out to purify your mind by cultivating the seeds of good deeds rather than just refusing to act wrongly then you can slowly become a truly virtuous human being. The method of Liao Fan, Franklin, Bettger or Carnegie should become your new way of living. Furthermore, you should set up a small shrine in your house (such as a section of a table) with an incense burner and any statues or images of sacred ideals to which you aspire. At the end of the day you light the stick of incense and formally/ritually report that day's efforts and progress to Heaven.

This is a daily practice I very much encourage in order to help people transform themselves. It is a method of ethical and moral reset that will uplift society and culture if practiced on a vast scale. Every individual and family should have a small table or shrine in front of which they can report their personal attempts at self-perfection and elevating their behavior (in the manner described by Franklin or Liao Fan) to Heaven for approval. This one practice alone will most definitely change the culture of a nation.

The family has the primary role to educate children in terms of character and behavior, and a school's job is to reinforce the positive behavior, character traits and values that the country and community deem proper. The family lays down the foundation of virtue and character, especially through the regularity of reaffirming family rituals, and the school builds upon that base. Teaching this inner watching method to children at home is therefore one means to help ethically reset the fiber of the nation.

Developing a Mental State Free of Attachments

---

[6] Napoleon Hill, *The Wisdom of Andrew Carnegie as Told to Napoleon Hill* (The Napoleon Hill Foundation, Virginia, 2004), pp. 64-65.

You can use many strategies to help you transform your mind and transition yourself to better behavior, but since the stream of errant mental afflictions is endless many policing strategies can end up tiring your willpower. What then do you do?

As taught, one of the highest mental attainments is to bypass the need for all these helpmates by actually emancipating the mind from all mental tendencies, freeing it from attachments to all mental habits, good and bad. To do this you must gradually cultivate a detached mental state through regular meditation and mindfulness practice so that eventually when negative thoughts arise you have enough mental powers to prevent them from transforming into negative behavior. Once again, you cultivate this degree of mental liberation through devoted meditation and mindfulness practice. We are normally bound to our thoughts, so mental liberation from their pull doesn't just happen without practice and training.

When thoughts arise that you do not want in regular life, you have to learn how to detach from them (or ignore them) so that they stop bothering you. By unhooking ourselves from thoughts by remaining as their observer who doesn't get entangled with them there is another great boon in addition to what we have already covered. This is the fact that we also bring ourselves closer to the world of direct experience.

Detachment and rationality are two of the highest methods for making your mind the tool it needs to be for life. They help us transcend the animal parts of our nature so that we can attain a higher stage of being and ennoble ourselves. In life you have to learn how to properly relate to your thoughts both good and bad. You have to learn how to deal with those that are unwanted, and generate the ones you need. The Confucian way teaches you how to do this.

A mind properly trained through meditation can remain balanced and unmoved in the presence of unwholesome thoughts or desires, and this is detachment. Detachment gives people the ability to ignore afflictions even though they may seem to overwhelm you. One remedy for dealing with the flooding of afflictive emotions, where you become extremely upset and physiologically aroused, is to call a time-out to the situation you are involved in. You might try to calm down by taking an intermission break and engage in other activities such as listening to music, practicing relaxation techniques, or other methods that prevent you from falling back upon automatic behavior once you've become flooded.

Mindfulness practice or inner watching develops your ability to detach from thoughts by having you shine awareness on them without becoming entangled with them. You practice observing thoughts, desires, attitudes, impulses and emotions without necessarily acting on them (without giving them extra energy) until this independent detachment becomes a habit. As a bonus, in time your mind will reach a higher state of inner quiet because of your disengagement and practice of defusing from them.

This practice doesn't mean that you adopt a laissez faire view of the world where nothing matters because you don't cling to your mental processes. It just means that you can create enough distance from thoughts when you need to be that way. Through detachment you can become an independent observer who can see them for what they are, and transcending them can make wiser choices than if entangled in their network. Of course when you need to practice focus and concentration you should still become fully engaged with thoughts as is necessary.

The point is that the spiritual path entails developing self-control to use thoughts but without succumbing to them so that they gain control over you. You are to always be their master. Detachment allows you to arise above your emotional, irrational or animalistic nature that usually masters you, and this will restore you to your rightful place as the ultimate master of your behavior.

As previously taught, the usual alternative to detachment is to use contemplation (wisdom analysis) to unwind attachment to thoughts and impulses, which is discriminative reasoning or comprehensive understanding, to help unravel the knots of afflictions at their root. Wisdom analysis involves more mental engagement, but usually produces a deeper and more long-lasting result when successful. Both methods must be practiced on the spiritual path.

Helping Society

We commonly lament that civic virtue has vanished in society and public morality has declined. The crux of the problem is that we do not emphasize self-improvement in society and so it has naturally become this way. All these methods of self-cultivation, for instance, remain unknown to the public yet are the most effective means for helping people in their lives.

Is not self-cultivation the right methodology for the moral reset of society? Should we not master both the automatic irrational as well as deliberate rational aspects of our mind, and bring mental control to fullest flower? Isn't this task, and its blossoming into virtuous behavior, what will make us fully human, noble or even divine?

In *Analects* 7.22 Confucius said, "Even when walking in a group of three companions, I will surely find instruction. I select what is positive from them and pursue it. I reflect upon what is negative and try to inwardly correct similar negative qualities that I might have." Once again, isn't this what we want everyone to do, which is to emulate the best we see in others but to use their negative qualities as a mirror for self-correction and self-improvement?

Confucius taught the practices of mindfulness, contemplation and self-improvement. His example once again demonstrates why you should take up the methods of Yuan Liao Fan and Benjamin Franklin since they embody this approach, elevating both the self and society. Their methods, which we should emulate as part of the Confucian way, entail the daily practice of watching your thoughts and monitoring your behavior by establishing a continuous mindfulness of inner observation. You can first develop this skill through sitting meditation practice that cultivates pristine awareness via witnessing, and then you can carry this skill into the regular world.

The Great Learning entails recognizing that you are separate from what your thoughts are saying and that you can change them to change your life. You can unhook or defuse yourself from thoughts rather than take them as absolute truths to be followed. You can use wisdom to override their pressure that often seems like a loud command demanding obedience.

The Confucian way, which actually involves adopting any or all of these techniques to help you transform your mind and behavior to whatever you want, will help you to stop investing in strong negative thoughts and detach from bad habit energies. By focusing on awareness, achieved through meditation and mindfulness training, one can transcend thoughts and become liberated from the contents of the mind.

The Confucian way of mindfulness helps you cultivate a clear clarity of mind that we call "being bright" because through this practice your mind will quiet of wandering nuisance thoughts. If you become perfectly clear about whatever are the contents of your mind, this is bright awareness or pristine awareness. It is not something new you create but something you always have. It is really just your ordinary mind. Using your bright awareness that is detached from the contents of the mind you will become able to transcend the habit of getting entangled with your thoughts, and by separating from your thoughts you can begin to transform your habit energies because of this independence.

Most types of schooling and education concentrate on teaching academic topics to children instead of training them how to cultivate bright awareness, how to properly use their minds to handle unwanted thoughts, or how to cultivate virtuous behavior through mental watching. Some countries even use their educational system to brainwash children with strange indoctrinations while leaving aside these most important lessons on virtuous character traits and how to control, use and develop the mind. Rather than academic topics that we'll forget, aren't these more important lessons for life? Don't we need to better learn how to fully control and use the mind?

Most often schools teach children how to develop mental skills such as logic, language, reasoning, communication and so on, which is found as a standard across the world. Yes, we do need to learn how to develop all the possible functions of the mind such as this and all the arts and skills necessary for survival and livelihoods. However, schools regularly fail to teach that we can silence afflictive thoughts and emotions when they arise in addition to the mental skills involved with intentional rational thinking. They fail to teach that our mind can control the body's internal energies too.

Since our thoughts can turn into outward behavior, in the end our education systems should teach children how to form better thoughts and transcend their animal natures so that they don't just blindly follow their urges and passions. They need to teach them how to use their mental capacities not just so that they can achieve excellent accomplishments, but so that they can achieve excellence in ethical behavior as well.

Unfortunately, schools don't teach the deep social message that a virtuous character is the basis of all trustworthy social interactions that students will eventually face in life. We can cultivate our character in order to become a noble, helpful actor in the larger world or an individual primarily consumed by the motivations of self-interest. People will know the difference through your behavior, and adjust themselves accordingly.

In *Analects* 4.15 we can discover which path Confucius preferred.

Confucius said, "Zeng! My Way is held together by a single strand." Master Zeng then replied, "Yes, certainly." After Confucius departed the other students asked Zeng what their teacher had meant and he replied, "The Master's Way lies in exerting all of one's effort and relating to the needs of others. That is all." This is the idea of compassion, giving or altruistic cooperation, which is the glue that binds together and uplifts societies. The idea is service to help others.

Our schools don't normally teach children how to detach from improper impulses. They simply command, "Don't do that." They don't teach the many ways we can transform unwholesome thoughts and habits into good ones either. They don't teach that people can cultivate virtue and goodness and even break bad habits through self-reflection, self-discipline and quiet sitting. They don't teach that one of the great goals in life is not necessarily worldly success, which can never be guaranteed, but the pursuit of serenity and the personal perfection offered by self-cultivation.

Our school systems teach children absolutely nothing about how to properly relate to their thoughts and emotions, especially unwanted ones. They don't teach the younger generation the specifics about how thoughts and emotions don't have to automatically determine their actions because they can always choose to generate and then follow higher ideals than whatever first appears in their mind. Despite all of us possessing habit energies of lower, baser inclinations children are never taught how to change their habit energies so that they are pointed toward more valuable directions.

As Confucius said in *Analects* 14.23, "Exemplary people reach higher, the petty descend lower," but do we teach children how to reach higher? Our educational systems focus on academic topics rather than moral topics. They don't teach children that they should strive to become exemplary individuals, admirable moral agents who will give their utmost to make a better world.

In order to operate well, greater society requires a community of virtuous, cooperative individuals who are together because they are willing to help one another. It requires individuals of righteous character who know good from evil and choose righteousness for their behavior rather than what is purely profitable. To produce such individuals we need educational systems that will stress character, and which teach children how to travel a road of self-perfection just as you have been taught. The

Confucian way does this and it is non-religious and non-denominational.

The foundation of your character is always established in your youth, and the habits you form in adolescence usually persist into adulthood. Even the twists and turns of your fate can usually be traced back to the character traits you developed in your youth. With this in mind, think about what and how you might teach children to give them the power to perfect their characters and fortunes.

The Confucian *Analects* are all about wise and proper living among others and getting good at life, which is why the principles within them are still valuable for modern living. However, they often focus on the larger picture without going into smaller remedies such as how to create a ledger system like Liao Fan's or Franklin's and how to handle some of the automatic negative processes of the mind. As a society we need to work at promoting knowledge of these various techniques in order to help people attain better self-mastery because self-improvement is the road to mental peace, accomplishment and prosperity.

These methods just reviewed are some of the many that can help us to master our minds when they consistently, automatically keep going astray despite our best efforts at mindfulness, inner viewing and detachment. By promoting them and the concept that we can and should learn to control/manage the automatic afflictions of the mind, we create a means for bringing about an ethical reset that society needs. They are the means of creating better communities everywhere because mastery of the mind leads to positive character traits and virtuous behavior.

Building a better world and benefitting others starts with building a better character. With a better character you have a greater chance to influence others and the world. These methods will give you some powerful ways to start getting control of your mind and dealing with thoughts properly so that you can improve your character and the power of your behavior. When mindfulness and meditation are not enough, you should use helpmates such as these to help eliminate afflictions and gain control over your mental processes, through which you can build the world.

CHAPTER 9:
DEALING WITH DEPRIVATION
AND DIFFICULT TIMES

Over the next century many men and women in developed nations will find themselves in the unfortunate state of perpetual unemployment. Globalization will have displaced many jobs to lower cost nations, and automation will have reduced employment opportunities as well. Joblessness will reign. The oil reserves of many petroleum nations will have run out collapsing their economies and producing poverty. Where there was once adequate employment opportunities, many people in what are now rich nations will face the agony of deprivation.

What can we expect during those future times of hardship and desperation? What should anyone do if their nation is faced with the terrible fortune of deprivation? We can turn to a story from the past to gain a few insights.

The great explorer Henry Morton Stanley, who charted the course of the Congo River in Africa, often took Europeans with him on his African expeditions. Typically two out of every three Europeans who went with him through Africa died along the way due to disease, starvation or attacks by natives.

At one time when he was leading his third expedition into Africa, Stanley made camp and then proceeded to venture into an uncharted rain forest by himself, leaving behind a rear column comprised of men from some of the most prominent families in Britain. What happened next may come as a surprise.

"Those men, along with a British soldier and doctor who were left in charge of a fort along the route, lost control once Stanley was no longer there to command them. They refused medical treatment to sick natives and allowed Africans under their command to perish needlessly from disease and poisonous food. They kidnapped and bought young African women to keep as sex slaves. When one of the very young concubines tried to be returned to her mother and father, she was ignored; when another escaped, she was retrieved and trussed to prevent another escape. The British commander of the fort savagely beat and maimed Africans, sometimes stabbing them with a sharp steel cane, sometimes ordering men to be shot or flogged almost to death for trivial offenses. Most of his officers raised no objection. When some Pygmies living near the British fort – a mother and several children – were caught stealing food, parts of their ears were cut off. Other thieves were shot and decapitated so that their skulls could be displayed as warnings outside the fort. One of officers in the Rear Column, a naturalist who was an heir to the Jameson whiskey fortune, paid for an eleven-year-old girl to be killed and eaten by cannibals – while he made sketches of the ritual."[7]

Stanley wrote of these men, "At home these men had no cause to show their natural savagery ... they were suddenly transplanted to Africa & its miseries. They were deprived of butcher's meat & bread & wine, books, newspapers, the society & influence of their friends. Fever seized them, wrecked minds and bodies. Good nature was banished by anxiety. Pleasantness was eliminated by toil. Cheerfulness yielded to internal anguish ... until they became but shadows, morally & physically of what they had been in English society." It is as Mencius once said, "In years of plenty many young men are reliable, but in years of want many cannot control themselves."

This descent into barbarity occurred because these men, despite having grown up in a highly civilized society, had not deeply internalized what Confucius called *li*, which are the socially expected rules of proper

---

[7] Roy Baumeister and John Tierney, *Willpower* (Penguin Books, London, 2012), pp. 142-143.

conduct and societal interaction that we must extend to even those we consider inferiors. Confucius's concept of *li* is often translated as "rites" or "rituals" but the meaning embodies a spirit of universal respect for others expressed through the norms of proper social behavior. *Li* represents the formalized, expected and therefore "ritualized" behaviors of a culture.

Li embodies the entire spectrum of human interactions within society, all of which should embody respect for others as the guide to personal conduct. It guides public expectations of proper behavior such as showing respect for one's parents, loyalty to one's superiors, trust to one's friends, integrity (honesty) with strangers and other factors related to social order.

In short, *li* represents proper behavior – rules of social etiquette and standards of personal conduct for the right way of doing things within relationships. It is preventive, for the principles of *li* are meant to turn a man away from evil before he has a chance to commit it.

Confucius taught that governing the masses should be based on concepts of *li* because the ideal is "to lead others by virtue and guide them with the rules of proper conduct." The principle of governing is that the concepts of virtue must be the highest standard so that people will know shame if they do something wrong, and wishing to avoid shame will become better people.

What is one such rule of *li*, or proper conduct? When Zigong asked Confucius what principle could serve for the conduct of life, Confucius answered "Perhaps the word 'reciprocity': Do not do to others what you would not want others to do to you." Rabbi Hillel, one of the most famous figures in Jewish history, said something similar, "That which is hateful to you, do not do to your fellow; this, in a few words, is the entire Torah; all the rest is just an explanation of this one, central point. Go and learn this." Whether Stanley's companions in Africa acted horrifically because they thought of themselves as superior to the natives, this central principle of behavior was something they definitely ignored.

Confucius said that correct behavior comes from internalizing culture while self-restraint comes from studying and mastering *li*, the standard forms of propriety through which one expresses respect for others. The problem demonstrated by these Europeans in Africa is that during difficult times they lost all forms of social self-restraint because they had not internalized a universal respect for others. They though of themselves as civilized, but they acted in quite the opposite fashion. Despite Christian upbringings, because they had not truly internalized *li* or *ren* ("loving people") they engaged in all sorts of barbaric acts. Their behavior was neither a Christian way nor the Confucian way.

In a future state of economic decline and deprivation, should we not expect this as well? Will people turn aside from ethics and virtue to engage in lies, thievery and even killing? Yes.

We personally choose how to treat other people in life. We have even instituted laws so that during a state of war we are to treat captured enemy combatants in a humane and decent manner. Their treatment as human beings deserving of respect, who are simply ordered to do whatever their country tells them to do, is based upon concepts of *li*. So that we do not revert to being animals, the higher principles of human propriety (*li*) are never to be discarded in life regardless of the difficulties of the situation.

There is a famous story of Confucius suffering great deprivation in the small Chinese state of Chen that we can compare to Stanley's African experience. The *Analects* records, "While in the state of Chen, food supplies for the journey were cut off. Followers fell ill and none was able to rise to his feet. Zilu saw Confucius and asked, 'Is it right that even the superior man should be reduced to poverty?' The Master replied, 'A superior man remains steadfast in the face of poverty; the small man, when impoverished, loses all restraint.'"

This is what we saw in Africa, and the question is whether many of us will hold to propriety if we face future difficult times of deprivation ourselves when economies sour and jobs disappear. When that happens, what is to be our guide for proper behavior other than just survival?

During the difficult times when we are tested we must strongly hold onto our concepts of *li*. Hindus and Buddhists tend to refrain from wrongdoing during difficult times because they are afraid of negative karma. Christian teachings are to always maintain a state of virtue and not fall into evil ways even if survival is at stake. Even so, all people who are reduced to having no income or food typically face a challenge to maintain proper behavior during times of want.

While Confucians also hold to the *Yijing's* principles of behavioral karma or merit for avoiding misfortune, Confucius simply said that we should hold to ethical, virtuous ways no matter what, even when life becomes horrifically awful. This is why Socrates also risked death under the Thirty Tyrants rather than abandon his principles.

Mencius also taught that we should maintain our strength of character to "have a constant heart" in the face of deprivation. At some time or another it is likely for us all to suffer some form of deprivation in life so the lessons are important. A Confucian is taught that he must learn to bear the pain with resilience, perseverance and determination to forge through it without losing his morals. He must tightly hold to the pathway of virtue while working through the deprivation and difficult times to change things for the better. A Confucian takes inner strength and invincible striving as the ideal model of behavior, which is to retain one's moral strength in the face of adversity.

It is not deprivation itself that leads us to abandon our sense of values when we are in need. People readily abandon their values when times become too difficult because their respect for virtue and proper ("ritual") behavior isn't strong enough.

Mencius warned, "The Way of the people is this: if they are full of food, have warm clothes, and live in comfort but are without instruction, then they come close to being animals." Men must be taught higher spiritual values for life that they should always maintain otherwise they will be no different than animals. Unfortunately, such instruction rarely holds during difficult times but only during times of plenty.

Spiritual cultivation and the Confucian way are all about rising above our animal nature, which medieval European alchemists called the irrational soul or impure soul of impulses and desires. To become truly human we must learn how to transcend our baser impulses, which some religions have called transcending our "lower self." This is how to realize our divinity. The spiritual path is a path that raises us above the animals, and thus it teaches us to become more humanitarian and altruistic rather than selfish or self-centered. Although you may imbibe, it is not a pathway of constantly following sensual desires.

Part of society's job is therefore to help people develop strong internal values through education, which is a responsibility that has traditionally been accomplished by the family and religion. Without family teachings and religion - the traditional mainstays of morality - can we expect the state to do this *correctly*? The answer is no, for while schooling can and should play a role of building on the foundation that families and religion build, the state will surely subvert the teachings for its own self-interest. Such is the history of the world. Once again, it is primarily the duty of religion, the family, and community to teach children ethics, morality, virtuous ways and strong values.

The ethical and moral reset required of society necessitates that the family assume a stronger role in educating children, next religion (where parents should override what is not proper from ancient religious codes being carried forward), and then communities. The ideal is to strengthen the ties within the family and community, especially by reaffirming rituals of family and neighborhood unity, and inculcate the civic notion to work and sacrifice for the common good. The entire burden of moral education should not be put on the schools.

While our own lives may involve a constant striving for better conditions for ourselves and others in a difficult environment, we must never neglect the importance of positive character training for our children, for they are to eventually build a new society. Our children are fated to create the future prosperity of our nations and they need character to do so. Despite the many difficulties and challenges we will face in our own lives, we must always focus on rising above baser ways of being. We must ennoble ourselves through devotion to proper conduct and the cultivation of virtues. This is how we build character, and is something we must demonstrate to our children through our own example.

How do we do this? How do we pursue a pure mind and pure behavior through difficult times? Confucius once commented, "The noble person who studies broadly in culture and restrains themselves through proper conduct will not go astray. (*Analects* 6.27)" An exemplary man - a man dedicated to perfecting his behavior through cultivation - studies culture and restrains himself through rules of propriety so that he won't jump the track when confronted with deprivation. Poor and destitute, one can still remain noble. The opposite is what had happened to these British men whom we would normally expect to have embodied the highest levels of culture despite their circumstances.

To become a truly virtuous person you must be taught to really *think* about what is really moral rather than just memorize rules of conduct like the Ten Commandments. Everyone needs to develop their own personal code of ethics for life, but it requires thinking to do so. You have to become committed to a moral path after deep reasoning, such as the "skillful means" moral pathway of Buddhism.

Everyone is a member of a family and local community. Also, we all have a regional, national and then civilizational identity. You derive your personal code of conduct through the influence of all these relationships - through the teachings of your family and religion and community, through personal experience and by thinking through the consequences of whatever you are about to do. This is how you can create a personal behavioral code for yourself.

Confucius said, "Against the rites (*li*), do not speak; against the rites, do not act." The idea is, "against the rites, do not look; against the rites, do not listen." In other words, find your code of behavior, practice that proper behavior and do not stray from what is proper. "Rites" does not mean rituals or ceremonies but the proper way for doing things in any situation according to the proper etiquette of social interaction. It stands for the formalized (accepted as proper) virtuous behaviors of a culture.

Rules of Conduct

Confucius also said, "Conquering yourself and returning to *li* constitutes Goodness. If for one day you could conquer yourself and return to *li* (proper behavior), the world would respond to you with Goodness. The key to achieving Goodness lies within yourself—how could it come from others? (*Analects* 12.1)"

What might those principles of Goodness be? What are the principles of exemplary behavior that constitute the "consummate conduct" of which Confucius speaks?

Throughout the ages men have endeavored to create proper ethical rules and moral philosophies on how we should interact with others. They proposed rules for behavior such as the conscience test (does this go against my conscience?), the consequences test (would this behavior create bad consequences?), the broadcasting test (what if everyone knew I did this?), the religion test (does this go against the rules of my religion?), the fairness test (is this fair to all the parties involved?), the "what if everybody did this?" test and all sorts of other tests to judge the properness of actions.

Along these lines Confucius espoused the ethical test of reversibility: "Don't do to others what you would not have them do to you." In other words, whenever somebody does something to another you should ask yourself whether you would be willing to accept this if it was done to you. When you measure the treatment of another by substituting yourself in the situation, whether it is proper or improper soon becomes clear. Thus the Golden Rule is to treat others as you would have them treat you with Rabbi Hillel's addition that "the rest is commentary."

On the ethics of behavior, Kant said that people should think about whether a rule guiding their actions and behavior could be proposed as a universal law, and thus arrived at the rule of universalizability: "Act in accordance with the maxim that your actions should become universal law." I personally feel that you should "move in the direction that most elevates you above your animal nature." Doug Casey proposed as the basic ethical rule of interactions, "Do not egress in any way against another person or their property." Chamfort (*Products of the Perfected Civilization*) said, "Enjoy and give pleasure, without doing harm to yourself or to anyone else – that I think, is the whole of morality."

The rule of John Wesley is to "Do all the good you can, in all the ways you can, in every place you can, at all the times you can, with all the zeal you can, to all the people you can, as long as ever you can." Buddhists espouse, "Do everything good you can, cut off any evil when you see it, don't block any unborn good from being born but never let unborn evil be born."

Since it seems almost impossible to establish a completely objective and universal set of ethical rules, it appears that the proper ethical rules to apply for any situation should be arrived at through careful reflection. This conclusion is embodied in the Mahayana principle of skillfulness where the ethics you are to apply to a situation are not rigid rules but flexible standards relative to the situation at hand.

Whatever the foundational rule we apply as our test of propriety, ethics and morality, we should remember the story where Master Zeng said, "The Master's Way lies in exerting all of one's effort and relating to the needs of others. That is all." Your actions in the world should be geared toward helping others.

There are many suggestions as to the fundamental moral principles that should guide everyone's life, and for years I searched for a fundamental few such as these that could serve as a single foundation. Everyone is searching for a fixed point, a center that will hold, and that center must involve foundational principles of behavior for your life. The Confucian way offers some suggestions for these principles, but the truth is that you must think deeply about these things to derive a clear code of conduct for yourself.

Even if you don't buy into the established shared value expectations (ritual conduct) of your country, culture, religion or family and friends, you still need to develop a set of standards for your own life, otherwise you have nothing at all to guide you. Developing such principles to guide your character and behavior is one of the expectations of Confucian cultivation. Finding those principles, adopting them into your life, and making your behavior conform to the higher standards you select is actually the road of all spirituality which religion is supposed to espouse.

Acting according to "ritual" (expected behavior) plays a constructive role on the road of Confucian self-cultivation because it helps you reshape your inner endowment towards a higher way of being, a more noble form of behavior. The "rites" perform a humanizing function of ennoblement by forcing you to practice conducting yourself as an exemplary being until that behavior becomes automatic. Only with awareness and understanding of what is proper, and then practice in effecting those proper forms of behavior, do we actually build the habits that ennoble us.

Until Confucius, a man acquired the status of being a gentleman or noble only through his birth into nobility. After Confucius's teachings became established in China, the correct idea took root that nobility was bestowed by merit rather than birth. You cultivated your behavior to develop cultural, spiritual and humanitarian values and thereby made yourself noble by your own effort. The nobility of blood was therefore replaced by the nobility of virtue and merit. This is one of the reasons that Confucius's teachings made a big impact on society throughout Asia. By elevating your own attitudes, thinking and behavior you raise yourself up and turn yourself into a gentleman, a noble, an exemplary being, a sage.

Confucius stated, "[human] natures are close to one another, but become far from one another by practice" (*Analects* 17.2). Because of exposure to different environments and because they repeatedly engage in certain types of good or bad behavior that become habitual, people slowly differ from purity and start to become shaped in different ways. Understanding this principle, which is that the environment is important for a child's upbringing, we can now understand why Mencius's mother moved three times. Her wisdom recognized the perfuming principle of slow permeation that slowly changes people's behavior for good or bad. The important question to therefore ask is this: since people become far from one another due to *practice*, with "becoming far from one another" meaning that some people choose lower roads that silence morality and ethics, what type of *practice* will ennoble people?

Mencius also said that human beings have a natural constitution that embodies certain emotional predispositions. He felt that each human being "inherently" has a heart with the capacity for positive virtues and it need only be developed. Education is supposed to do just this. The Confucian way is to believe that human nature is inherently good and that becoming a good person is the result of personally developing our innate tendencies toward benevolence, righteousness, and propriety. In other words, the Confucian way is that we can all become better through a road that teaches us to become one with our inherent goodness.

In other words, our natural predispositions already point in the direction of goodness, and because of those predispositions we are capable of perfecting ourselves even more if we have the benefit of a positive environment and training. This is the proper attitude to have in life for even when we seem to lack talent in some life area, training can develop our skills and abilities in a new direction of our choosing, and that includes the fields of virtue, morality and ethics.

Mencius felt that "becoming bad" is not the fault of one's constitution, but a matter of either injuring or not fully developing one's constitution in the appropriate direction. He also believed that through training by parents, relatives, teachers *and through personal self-cultivation* we can develop our innate capacities into fully formed virtues.

Daily Review

How then should you proceed to develop yourself to become better? The premier Confucian way is meditation practice and the mindfulness of self-correction, and Liao Fan and Benjamin Franklin showed how we can formalize this into a daily practice. Franklin once wrote of this technique, "On the whole tho' I never arrived at the perfection I had been so ambitious of obtaining, but fell far short of it, yet I was, by the endeavor, a better and a happier man than I otherwise should have been if I had not attempted it."

Franklin's attitude showed evidence of Mencius's growth mindset that your character virtues can definitely be developed in the direction that you want even if you never attain the final goal you seek. This is the correct attitude of mindfulness cultivation. Just as you struggle hard in twelve to twenty or more years of schooling to develop your intellectual potential, Franklin and Liao Fan showed that you must also struggle for positive character development by reducing the errors marring moral perfection. Hard it may be, but as Franklin said the effort is worth the journey.

The point of mindfulness is to identify personal faults and errors you have and to continuously monitor yourself to cut them off immediately whenever they appear. You are always to catch yourself and stop rather than continue doing what you see and know to be wrong. Throughout history the influence of religion and moral teachings have been the traditional means to redirect people away from non-virtue and teach them self-control, but this method of self-control is even higher. It is part of a culture of continuous improvement and it works because you are forced to track your personal progress to really see whether you are improving or not.

Science will tell us that the methods of Liao Fan and Benjamin Franklin will create positive changes in the brain, as does any sort of behavioral training, and those neural changes can help you alter your behavior permanently. The mindfulness method of observation they both employed is not only how we normally correct what's wrong with our behavior but also how we should develop our potential. It's how we can build skills in the virtues we want, but we need the determination of follow-through to do so.

Along this pathway of development, it is especially important to start cutting off behavioral errors that go against the virtues you want to instill in yourself. Franklin best showed that we can cut off errors in order to cultivate positive virtues. Liao Fan showed that we can also use self-observation to push ourselves to do good deeds. The right sort of mindful self-corrective practice carried out over a sufficient period of time will indeed lead to any type of improvement you want to engineer, and the methods we've revealed will certainly help you perfect yourself as Confucius recommended. No other techniques work as well as these.

The Weekly One Hour Review

In *Character Matters*, author Thomas Lickona even recommends that our schools organize a strategy for promoting virtues to children along the lines just covered. He suggests various curriculum options for teaching children such as promoting one virtue a month, a virtue per week, a three-

or four-year teaching cycle of virtues, a yearly theme of virtue, a developmentally appropriate virtue emphasis per grade level, and so on. A point to take home from his plan is that character development ought to involve a continuous effort to develop moral potential.

Whether at home or at school, I strongly recommend that we teach Franklin's method of concentrating on one virtue per week, or Liao Fan's method of daily watching your mind to promote good deeds as well as cut off faults. I also recommend people be taught that the Daily Review Method should be supplemented by a One-Hour Per Week review of your progress *and your life* as detailed in my book *Quick, Fast, Done*.

The practice of spending an hour per weekend reviewing that week's efforts at self-cultivation (or the events of the week in general) will give you a chance to step back and re-assess how you are living and what you are really doing in life. A weekend review provides you with the opportunity to introspect and see a larger picture, and by regularly practicing this type of awareness you can learn how to step out of the stream of your daily affairs to improve your life and bring it back on track whenever necessary. This method of weekly review will allow you to reach the highest stages of moral development and personal accomplishment.

In *How to Win Friends and Influence People* Dale Carnegie told the story of the president of an important Wall Street bank who admitted that he owed most of his career success to reviewing his life for just one hour every week. The banker, addressing one of Carnegie's classes on self-improvement, described his method:

"For years I have kept an engagement book showing all the appointments I had during the day. My family never made any plans for me on Saturday night, for the family knew I devoted a part of each Saturday evening to the illuminating process of self-examination and review and appraisal. After dinner I went off by myself, opened my engagement book, and thought over all the interviews, discussions and meetings that had taken place during the week. I asked myself:

"'What mistakes did I make that time?'

"'What did I do that was right – and in what way could I have improved my performance?'

"'What lessons can I learn from that experience?'

"I often found that this weekly review made me very unhappy. I was frequently astonished at my own blunders. Of course, as the years passed, these blunders became less frequent. Sometimes I was inclined to pat myself on the back a little after one of these sessions. This system of self-analysis, self-education, continued year after year, did more for me than any other one thing I ever attempted.

"It helped me improve my ability to make decisions—and it aided me enormously in all my contacts with people. I cannot recommend it too highly."

Taking one hour per week to review your previous week's activities, such as your self-improvement efforts, is a great way to help you stay in line with your core values, help you eliminate any habitual errors you have been making in life, and accomplish your life goals. It falls directly in line with the Confucian method of daily self-observation.

In his book *Make it Big! 49 Rules for Building a Life of Extreme Success,* the real estate developer Frank McKinney explained how he would take time off every weekend to proactively review his life and his business in the manner discussed:

"Every Saturday afternoon … I sit down with the previous week's chart and a copy of my personal vision statement. I review my vision statement first, to remember the big picture of what I want my life to be about this year. Then I look at the previous week's accomplishments and what hasn't gotten done, and I ask, 'How was this week? How did I approach things? What did I do well? What did I do wrong? Where did I fail, not only professionally but personally? Where did I not live up to my personal vision statement?' Then I ask the most important questions: 'What can I learn from this? How can I be a better person next time?' I write the answers to all those questions on the back of the previous week's chart. Once I have done my introspection, then—and only then—am I ready to plan a new week. Weekly introspection gives me the ability to grasp everything that's going on around me and, for the most part, to feel in control of the direction of my life."[8]

This type of weekly review, which will help you gain an accurate perspective on your life, should certainly be performed regulaly. Everyone needs to set aside a regular time where they perform some self-reflection and evaluate how well they have lived the past week, month, quarter or year or whatever the time period being considered. This will make the

---

[8] Frank McKinney, *Make It Big! 49 Secrets for Building a Life of Extreme Success* (John Wiley & Sons, New York, 2002), pp. 31-32.

mindfulness technique much more powerful. If you make this a regular ritual you can use it to substantially improve your life and help you keep on track towards achieving what you wish to accomplish. This will help you achieve your aspirations for creating an outstanding life.

In line with these same principles you might consider the following methods to help strengthen your family. Consider instituting weekly Family Get Together days such as regular family movie nights, Sunday brunch, or some other regular weekly function. A regular ritual might involve a weekly date night with your spouse or a weekly get together where they jointly pay their bills and talk about their finances. You might even establish regular rituals with people whose presence in your life is part of your greater life goals such as a workout buddy, close friends, a Mastermind group of like-minded business associates, etc.

Regular family traditions will bring about a feeling of family unity and closeness. This type of regular activity, which offers a potential period for *meaningful communication* between everyone, can strengthen family bonds tremendously. Most families already have their own periodic traditions such as a yearly Thanksgiving dinner, Christmas season get-together, regular Sunday meal, and other special occasions. We should always try to maintain such traditions, even during periods of deprivation, because they are necessary for the development of a close-knit family.

Reading to your children or discussing moral tales or intellectual topics with them, such as at the dining table, are other ways to influence them towards virtuous behavior. These types of activities not only build moral character but build the family too. By interacting strongly with your children on a regular basis you can influence them to develop special interests and proper conduct, which is the Confucian way. The more positive interactions you have with them to guide them, and the more meaningful conversations you have with them to help them develop their independent thinking processes, the more you can protect them from the pressures, bad examples and temptations they will regularly find outside of the home.

Public Holidays and Ceremonies

Family gatherings held on a regular, rhythmical basis add to the seasonality of life, put meaning on the passage of time, and their feelings of togetherness create group comfort and security. They create wonderful lasting memories for everyone that help solidify family culture and bind members closer together. They impart cohesion to the family, connect us with our past, and help families shape a sense of shared identity and values. In short, the regularity of family traditions helps to build successful families. We need this to build strong ethical communities. This is all part of the Confucian way.

Holidays and large societal gatherings (ritual) have the magical power to cooperatively integrate disparate elements of communities and larger society into one harmonious whole for a short period of time. They fulfill our need to feel a transcendent whole that is great and harmonious within. At those times people will often share a unified body of emotions; even the non-religious might partake of great feelings of unity, closeness, elevation, awe, sublimity or grandeur. Thus public holidays can create a cooperative positive culture that can uplift (transform) people's characters for the better. Such large get-togethers also belong to Confucius's concept of rites or rituals and their ability to transform people.

It is a powerful technique to use the method of perfuming as a means of cementing national unity. Public holidays and ceremonies fall into the category of annual perfuming activities for developing national cohesion. They help create a "high-purpose environment" that can unify disparate peoples into a single purpose. On this Daniel Coyle said, "Purpose isn't about tapping into some mystical internal drive but rather about creating simple beacons that focus attention and engagement on the shared goal. Successful cultures do this by relentlessly seeking ways to tell and retell their story. To do this, they build what we'll call high purpose environments.

"High purpose environments are filled with small, vivid signals designed to create a link between the present moment and a future ideal. They provide the two simple locators that every navigation process requires: *Here is where we are* and *Here is where we want to go*."[9] This type of strategy can be nationally applied for the objective of aiming a country in a particular direction and creating stronger national unity along those lines.

High-purpose environments deliver an unbroken array of consistent little signals, and the total environment of perfuming they create can lead a person or people to some greater degree of morality, altruism, cooperation and wellbeing. Holidays and national ceremonies, when skillfully administered, can therefore help accomplish difficult things like producing

---

[9] Daniel Coyle, *The Culture Code* (Random House, London, 2018), pp. 180-181.

national unity, internal peace, wealth and greatness.

All societies need the regeneration created when disparate elements of society harmoniously come together for holidays, and other periods of communal excitement. The sentiments shared by the group are larger than what an individual can normally experience on his own, and feeling that great energy everywhere is transformative in building cohesive community spirit. People who participate in the event can feel the overwhelming energy of the group spirit in a cooperative mode, which helps to stimulate emotions and transform society.

Most nations have developed on the basis of farming and agriculture. Many community celebrations and festivals therefore occur just after harvest season when the crops of the field are normally brought in. At that time, farming families usually possess an abundance of riches (the crops they have grown), which typically gives rise to a great moment of joy where generosity is shared throughout society because of the abundance. Such moments help unify society by creating a shared sense of community.

Do we not need a sense of shared national unity where we live, or do we want identity politics that aim to split a nation apart? History clearly shows that splits within nations are often carefully orchestrated by various parties in order to weaken or destroy the country. Many times they are promoted behind the scenes by some minor group so that it can gain power. We must teach people to think for themselves so that they can see when this is happening rather than remain blind to such events and subject to manipulation.

Are we so gullible as to let deviant forces gain such control that they can destroy the cooperative integration of society? Confucius warned strongly against letting this happen for many of his teachings are about cooperation and social cohesion. Communities are built through social cohesion which is in turn built upon cooperative social harmony. The leadership helm of a country is at fault if it ever lets the social glue weaken.

Along these lines, public holidays and ceremonies can be used to counteract such trends by cementing a feeling of harmonious unity and goodwill within communities and the larger whole. All of us should desire that the social bonds within our nation get stronger rather than fracture because people start emphasizing differences rather than community.

Unfortunately, America has been guided over the past few decades by a cabal of liberal intellectuals with strange ideas of social engineering that don't work, but which are actually fracturing and destroying the country. It is as if they have been undermining America on purpose. Their ideas and influence have been so bad that one can only suspect that they have a hidden agenda to actually fragment the nation into bitter factions, create endless internal war and marginalize traditional culture, perhaps because they believe it will allow them to gain even more power or ultimate control. Many intellectuals wrongly promoted Communism in the past hoping they would become leaders within the new power bloc, thus illustrating this mistake. Along these lines, certain groups have certainly organized with the intent to destroy America and its traditional values, but the narrative is being controlled to hide this fact and silence any criticism of the efforts.

Because of the importance of national unity, the diseases and aberrations of the social body are not to be trumpeted everywhere as normal occurrences either, nor are everyday life and commonsense views to be made into perversions. This is not the Confucian way. For national renewal, people must come to their senses and stop allowing this type of nonsensical messaging. Integrity and harmonious cooperation must once again become promoted throughout any society that wants internal peace and affluent prosperity.

The Importance of National Unity

Confucius taught many lessons on promoting national unity, and the Confucian emphasis on virtue and mindfulness plays a role in this objective. Every nation should try to create an internal shared vision and purpose with a high collective solidarity that brings out the country's magnificence.

People instinctively experience an "Attraction to the Great" and want to connect themselves to something bigger than themselves in life. They want a life purpose larger than themselves and want to associate with ideals or movements greater than themselves too. They want to feel a sense of unity from being at one with something that is grand and uplifting. They want to feel like they are part of something big and important. They want to connect to a larger story, a unifying vision, a broader current rather than just the typical human life cycle of birth, adolescence, middle age, senior times and then death. They want to feel part of something bigger than themselves and surrender to that bliss. This is why national holidays are important, and national unity too.

In order for a small group to take over the leadership helm of a nation it must employ well-used methods from the playbook of history to destroy its unity. For example, it must strive to weaken the population by breaking its internal ethnic unity (or other types of cohesive unity) which it will try to accomplish by emphasizing differences. It must employ immigration to flood a country with foreigners in order to replace the current population and dilute its strong identity. It must promote identity politics, dissension and hatred to create factions since it is a small group itself, and once there are many factions it can rise from among them to rule.

A smaller group needs multiple factions to protect itself, which is why it promotes them even when they are radical. Once established it will use the strategy of divide and conquer to destroy any groups that oppose its rise if it truly wants to take over the leadership helm. All these efforts involve destroying national unity to gain control. An aspiring group will never stop trying to move its agenda forward even if it takes decades, doing everything possible to destroy the ancient sovereignties of the people. This is the common pattern of history.

Such groups hate independent people as well as any populations who can resist them, so they try to destroy traditional cultures in order to gain control of everyone. Once they obtain the weapons of any people who might resist them (thus decreasing the military power of potential opponents) they typically move to crush a population, take away property rights and put a country under totalitarianism. If not in complete control, a group will simply fracture national unity, using the methods discussed, to gain dominant control while leaving the governmental system in place.

This is the strategic playbook that a smaller group, perhaps a tribal minority, often uses to gain control, domination and subjugation of a larger population. It is a strategy that wipes away national traditions and religion and embeds animosity in order to create and sustain segregation rather than to promote a national unity of shared values.

All this is against the Confucian way. To avoid becoming a victim, such strategies must always be seen for what they are although they are often disguised by lofty words and their uncovering is actively opposed. You must cultivate wisdom and *clear awareness* to see what is really going on in order to oppose this type of effort. This is one of the reasons you are taught to cultivate clarity, wisdom and awareness.

President Putin of Russia once gave an indication of the proper attitude for protecting a country when he spoke about minorities who wished to live in Russia. Putin said, "Any minority, from anywhere, if it wants to live in Russia, to work and eat in Russia, it should speak Russian, and should respect the Russian laws. For instance, if they prefer Sharia Law, and want to live the life of Muslims then we advise them to go to those places where that's the state law. Russia does not need minorities. Minorities need Russia, and we will not grant them special privileges, or try to change our laws to fit their desires, no matter how loud they yell 'discrimination.' We will not tolerate disrespect of our Russian culture."

The deep message within the *Analects* also concerns bringing about national unity. Confucius taught that the goal of a great society is for the people to interact harmoniously and cooperatively in one whole, but today across the world certain groups are working to internally fracture many nations in order to dominate or destroy them. They work to collapse the social bonds between people with the target of destroying national sovereignty so that the countries might be controlled by other parties. They work to erode and eviscerate the national fiber within many countries step-by-step in order to gain power themselves or turn the country into a collectivist system controlled by others. Despite their utopian promises, the only way to ensure real peace and prosperity for people is to avoid divisiveness and pursue the unity message conveyed within the *Analects*.

The strategies used by groups intent on dividing and conquering, using "diversity," "white supremacy" and religion or other means to hide their true intentions, would be strongly censured by Confucius. In *Analects* 14.42 Confucius said, "The exemplary man cultivates himself by bringing calm to the people – even a sage king such as Yao or Shun would be challenged in that regard." If even sage kings would be challenged in trying to bring internal peace to a country, how can a strategy of fragmentation help a nation? It will either destroy a country or lead to radical power-hungry minorities gaining control, and once in control they will repress others and destroy the national fabric.

Confucius taught much on how to properly rule a country. For instance, Confucius was not worried about poverty and deprivation but instability in a nation. He did not worry about underpopulation but about unevenly distributed income because a large income disparity between the elites and the populace usually leads to a revolution and overthrow of the government.

When wealth is poorly distributed within a country then there will be poverty. The cure is a strong middle class and policies that end up storing the country's wealth among the people. If the leaders work to do this while creating national unity and harmony then the chances of overturning the government through revolution - an event seen countless times in history - will be prevented.

Today there is a worldwide attack against nationalism, but what can replace the mechanism of social solidarity and unity consciousness provided by patriotism? If you say religion then you must realize that unseen forces within many countries are also striving to weaken religion in order to gain control of those nations. Yes, they strive to weaken religion in order to promote their own agenda! Therefore we cannot always rely on religion to help, but we might be able to rely upon clear awareness to see the attempts at destruction and thwart them. You already know the Confucian method for cultivating such clarity.

A country needs to develop a unity of mentality that holds the whole together and unites people through social cohesion. Every nation needs to make a very strong effort to educate its people about the spirit of real patriotism, cooperation, civic participation and national unity so that divisionary forces can be resisted despite however nice they are dressed up. Everyone must be encouraged to love their country and work for its development.

There is a great benefit when a nation's free citizenry sustain their inner lives with a *voluntary* vision of national magnificence to which they can subscribe even if the country is poor and suffering deprivation. That vision must something greater than found in mundane life so that people can find gratification in elevating themselves to that higher standard, even if for only a short while. At the same time the people must see that the government is helping them work towards that better future.

The entire line of thought in the *Analects* is that deprivation is not to be feared. What we should fear is that we do not cultivate moral wholeness during that time and keep working to make things better. Confucius said in *Analects* 2.3: "Guide the people with virtue, keep them in line with expected behavioral norms and they will, besides having a sense of shame, reform themselves." This is true.

Feeding the people, argued Confucius, is not the most important thing in managing a country. What's important is that the ruler becomes known as embodying virtue so that the people trust him and not lose faith in him or the government even during deprivation. A simple story illustrates this.

When Tzu-kung engaged Confucius in a conversation about governance Confucius said that you should give the people enough food, and defense (arms) and then they will have trust in you as a leader. Tzu-kung then asked him, "If you had to give up one of these three (food, protection or trust), which should you give up first?" Confucius replied, "Give up arms." Tzu-kung then asked, "If one had to give up one of the remaining two, which should one give up first?" Confucius answered, "Give up food. The reason is because death (due to lack of food) has always been with us since the beginning of time, but when there is no trust, the common people will have nothing to stand on." In other words, when managing a country the major concern is not prosperity when a nation starts out poor. Rather, the concern is having leaders whom the people can trust, for you need great leadership to lead you out of poverty.

Just as we learned from Stanley's men in Africa who abandoned their values during a state of deprivation, here Confucius reminded us that death is always with us but this is preferable to abandoning your values. Socrates, who chose to drink poison hemlock rather than depart Athens to save himself from certain death, also taught the same lesson - holding to your values by refraining from doing wrong was more important than death or deprivation. When the members of society are unwaveringly devoted to pursuing virtuous ways despite the difficulties then the result is that they will produce a culture that is maximally great, even if it has to suffer through states of deprivation.

The message is simple. Society as a whole may become poor or destitute, as is presently seen in many countries of the world and has been seen throughout history, but that is not the important thing. The important thing is that a people must deeply cultivate culture and ethical values as strive to push things forward. They must never forgo their sense of culture and values because of their current poverty. In fact, deprivation calls for an even greater need for altruistic behavior and community cooperation rather than selfishness. The worst that can ever happen to a population is to die, which is a natural thing that happens to everybody, but if we discard our values because of poverty we become nothing but mere animals.

The principle actually being taught in the conversation between Confucius and Tzu-kung is that a government should exhibit a strong enough moral basis that the people will trust it even if the country encounters difficulty. From time to time calamities will happen in countries - such as plagues, floods, famines, economic catastrophes or war - but the biggest worry is that the government should lose the trust of its people. This is when progress comes to a halt because of poor leadership.

If the people are to trust the government through times of difficulty they must see that the officials are commonly acting ethically, and this can only happen if ethical values are deeply embraced by society. How do you spread such values through a society? This feat is accomplished through a nationwide emphasis on proper behavior starting in families, in the schools and religion. It derives from a public emphasis on self-correction through self-reflection, an emphasis on good citizenship and civic responsibility, and an emphasis on shared traditions and forward efforts. Confucius also felt that elevating art and music had the power to transform human nature in the direction of virtue by ennobling the human heart. Therefore what the nation chooses to elevate in art and music will have a deep effect on its national character as well.

If we want to bring about an ethical and moral reset for a country, people need to take these ideas to heart and stew on them. Only if all the people are taught to pursue virtue will government officials have a natural tendency to pursue virtuous ways even in the darkest of times. When infractions occur they must be prosecuted because there is no limit to the ruthlessness and murderous cruelty that some men will engage in to seize money or power if they go unchecked. The good must therefore restrain evil rather than put up with it. This is usually a distasteful task that the virtuous abhor, but this is a necessity.

If the populace sees that good is rewarded and evil punished, it will remain committed to the road of virtue during difficult times. The people and government will together be able to work together to pull themselves out of deprivation. Countries are built upon a foundation of internal cooperation for the public good. When a people decide to put aside selfish motives to pursue a higher mission of helping the country then it will move forward in strides and bounds. You can encourage this by stressing the Confucian way.

CHAPTER 10:
ERRANT MEN OF BUSINESS

The very opening of the book of Mencius starts out with a special conversation. It is between Mencius and King Hui of Liang, who greeted Mencius saying,

> 'Sir [Mencius], … You have come all this distance, thinking nothing of a thousand li. You must surely have some way of profiting my state?'
>
> 'Your majesty,' answered Mencius, 'What is the point of mentioning the word "profit"? All that matters is that there should be benevolence and rightness. If Your Majesty says, "How can I profit my state?" and the Counselors say, "How can I profit my family?" and the Gentlemen and Commoners say, "How can I profit my person?" then those above and those below will be trying to profit at the expense of one another and the state will be imperiled. When regicide is committed in a state of ten thousand chariots, it is certain to be by a vassal with a thousand chariots, and when it is committed in a state of a thousand chariots, it is certain to be by a vassal with a hundred chariots. A share of a thousand in ten thousand or a hundred in a thousand is by no means insignificant, yet if profit is put before rightness, there is no satisfaction short of total usurpation. No benevolent man ever abandons his parents, and no dutiful man ever puts his prince last. Perhaps you will now endorse what I have said, "All that matters is

that there should be benevolence and rightness. What is the point of mentioning the word 'profit'?"[10]

Consider this: If the ruler of a country is motivated primarily by profits (money) then how can he expect higher ideals from anyone else in his own kingdom? Mencius, like Confucius, therefore emphasized virtue and ethics over the pursuit of personal wealth and advantage. A well-known truth is that when greed and corruption are seen among the country's elites it tends to foster greed and corruption at all lower levels of society.

There is a story about the reaction of the Grand Historian of China when he read this passage:

As the Grand Historian was reading Mencius, he unconsciously put the book down and sighed when he came to the place where King Hui of Liang asked Mencius, 'How will you profit my country?' The historian said, 'Ah, profit is truly the beginning of disorder. That is why Confucius seldom spoke of profit, always shoring up the source.' The source is the beginning. Whether it is found among the upper classes or the lower classes, the degeneracy of lust for profit is basically the same. When those in public office profit unfairly, then the law is disordered. When those in the private sector profit by deception, then business is disordered. When business is disorderly, people are contentious and dissatisfied; when law is disorderly, the citizenry is resentful and disobedient. This is how people get to be so rebellious and belligerent that they don't care if they die. Is this not a demonstration of how, 'Profit is truly the beginning of disorder'? The sages and saints were deeply cautious and aloof from profit, giving honor and precedence to humanity and justice. But in later times there were still those who deceived each other in hopes of profit; what limit is there to those who destroy morality and ruin education? How much the more serious is the problem when the path of adventurous profiteering is publicly espoused and pursued; under these conditions, how could we hope for the

---

[10] *Mencius, Volume One*, transl. by D. C. Lau (The Chinese University Press, Hong Kong, 1984), p. 3.

world's morals and customs to be upright, and not be thin and weak?[11]

We cannot assure ourselves of anything in life such as the attainment of riches, power or honors. Therefore throughout the *Analects* Confucius continually stressed that self-cultivation should take preference over the pursuit of wealth, salary or profits:

The Master said, "Exemplary persons make their plans for the sake of the Way and not for the sake of sustenance. Tilling the land often leads to starvation as a matter of course; studying often leads to an official salary as a matter of course. The exemplary person worries about the Way, not about poverty." (*Analects* 15.32)

The exemplary man understands what is moral. The small man understands what is profitable. (*Analects* 14.23)

Wealth and high station are what men desire but unless I got them in the right way I would not remain in them. Poverty and low station are what men dislike, but if they cannot be avoided while staying in accordance with the Way you should not try to avoid them. (*Analects* 4.5)

The Master said, "To eat coarse food, drink plain water and pillow oneself on a bent arm - there is pleasure to be found in these things. But wealth and position gained through inappropriate means are to me like floating clouds." (*Analects* 7.16)

The exemplary man (gentleman) seeks neither a full belly nor comfortable lodgings. (*Analects* 1.14)

There is no point in seeking the views of a gentleman who,

---

[11] Nan Huai-Chin, *The Story of Chinese Zen* (Charles E. Tuttle Company, Vermont, 1985), pp. 205-206.

though he sets his heart on the Way, is ashamed of poor food and poor clothes. (*Analects* 4.9)

The Master said, "Exemplary persons cherish their excellence; petty persons cherish their land. Exemplary persons cherish fairness; petty persons cherish the thought of gain." (*Analects* 4.11)

The Confucian Cheng Yi (1033–1107) said, "A gentleman never fails to desire profit, but if one is single–mindedly focused on profit then it leads to harm. If there is only benevolence and righteousness then one will not seek profit, but one will never fail to profit."

Let us be clear about this topic because no one can live life without self-interest in mind. Self-interest should definitely lead us to want to profit ourselves, and we should definitely pursue profits if we have a job or business otherwise we will have no income or way to survive. The real lesson is to undertake this pursuit of profits *in the right way*.

The principles is that in seeking profits we should never abandon our ethical values by forgetting self-cultivation and what it ultimately entails. Every profession, for instance, has its own identity, mission, best practices and standards. In executing your job or profession, just as it has its own standards you too must remain true to your own values and standards.

The cruelty we see in nature of animals eating one another finds an equivalence in the world of men. That equivalence is men battling one another in single-minded pursuit of selfish interests (profit) without regards to humanity. Men will turn to corruption, lawlessness and go as far as even raping, crippling or killing others to pursue status, power and profits. Men must therefore insist on safe checks against rampant abuse by others and learn to police their own behavior so that they do not become as cruel as animals in pursuing self-interests.

Just as the economy cannot be the be-all and end-all of life, a society cannot be based on pursuing profits alone. It must instead pursue the achievement of prosperity and harmonious happiness that embodies a wide variety of creative interests and a high measure of cultural advance.

Errant Men of Business

Profits do not lead to spiritual redemption. However, many men become seduced by profits because they represent the potential to fulfill any desired appetite and give avenue to the animalistic drive for power. If a man so pursues profits that he abandons his humanity then like Ebenezer Scrooge he becomes an "errant man of business."

What is an "errant man of business"? It is someone who compromises professionalism, ethics and humanism in pursuit of profits. They may look like gentlemen and outstanding members of society but errant men of business have put aside their souls, their humanity and responsibility to fellow humans in pursuit of just money. Here are some blatant examples of "errant men of business" who were willing to commit gigantic crimes that harmed other human beings just for the pursuit of money.

When the executives of cigarette companies maintained that there was no relationship between smoking and cancer, attempted to engineer cigarettes to become maximally addictive by manipulating nicotine levels, and stood in front of Congress testifying that they firmly believed cigarettes were not addictive, they proved themselves as errant men of business. They choose profits over lives.

When Nestle executives distributed the company's baby formula to nursing mothers in the Third World for free, it gave just enough so that lactating mothers would have their milk dry up. Mothers and their babies became entirely dependent on the formula, which they could not afford to purchase after the trial period, and thus thousands of babies died. Through this deed alone in order to increase sales, Nestle executives became errant men of business.

When vaccine manufacturers deny that there is any link between using vaccines and damage (such as autism) when evidence strongly indicates otherwise, they become errant men of business who choose unethical profits over human lives. In 1987 Smith-Kline Beecham released a vaccine in Canada, Triverix, that caused meningitis. Forced to stop selling the vaccine in Canada, it changed the name to Pluserix and sold the vaccine in the UK, again causing an outbreak of meningitis. Forced to stop selling the vaccine in the UK, it then sold the vaccine in Brazil and caused another meningitis outbreak. When executives act in this manner they are errant men of business.

When Monsanto sued farmers because its own GMO products contaminated their fields, its lawyers and executives became errant men of business. The company in thousands of actions has shown that its executives have positioned it incorrectly in the moral universe. In many arenas Monsanto has clearly demonstrated that when profits become the only destination that matters then people will often choose the low road to get there.

When investment banking employees mislead their clients to sell them shitty products to clean their books and then bet against those same products they just sold to "suckers," they become errant men of business. When the executives of Goldman Sachs perjured themselves before Congress about the doings of their firm (claiming that they were not significantly net-short the mortgage market when their own position was internally called "the big short" that accounted for 54% of the bank's risk) they also became errant men of business.

The top salesmen at many firms regularly lie to their clients all the time through exaggeration and omission in order to make sales and stay employed. They too have become errant men of business.

Many other examples can be given of lawyers, lobbyists, government officials and politicians who lost their moral center in the pursuit of profits, namely self-interest. Many corporations, given the blessing of making "legal profits," would readily suck the blood out of any humans until they killed all of humanity. For the United States, one of the kisses of death that accelerated this reign of terror appeared when it gave corporations the same rights as individuals and allowed them to contribute to political campaigns, thus sealing the fate of its citizenry to be treated as unchecked plunder. The U.S. did not design its system towards just ends. It forgot that people are primary, not corporations, and there should be principles to follow that are higher than making money.

Higher than pursuing profits is staying true to humanistic values, offering benefit to others while doing the right thing in all situations even though profits might entice you to do otherwise. This is a humanistic principle ignored by modern profit-seeking corporations. The principle of the Confucian way, on the other hand, is to live a moral life that contributes to communities rather than preys on society by sucking out profits through unethical or immoral means.

"Success" or "station" in life are typically measured by extreme wealth, power, station or prestige. However, Confucius reframed the importance people normally held for this type of success by recasting success in terms of a man's behavior. He focused our efforts on becoming what has been translated as virtuous individuals, gentlemen of benevolence, exemplary men and women, or men and women of consummate conduct. Whether or not you become an exemplary man or woman is determined by whether you are living according to the highest ethical values.

Confucius shook the ancient world by storm for he taught that the noble was not a man born into nobility but someone who became exemplary because of their consummate conduct. He thereby put nobility within everyone's reach by labeling the measuring stick as one's behavior.

The Confucian way recognizes that people do not always achieve their goals in life such as their dreams to become powerful or financially wealthy. For instance, only one person can become the winner of a sports tournament, the biggest in their industry or top of their class. Therefore, people must pursue a universal goal achievable by all where everyone can become winners. Pursuing consummate conduct, which is part of the Great Learning, must become that preeminent goal rather than the pursuit of perishable and perhaps unachievable profits, assets and other selfish interests.

Epictetus and Stoicism

Interestingly enough, the Greek philosopher Epictetus also taught that the highest prize in life was not assets, position or power but serenity and peace of mind, and that self-mastery over our desires and emotions lead to this spiritual peace. Accordingly he said that we should not focus on "revenues or income, or peace or war, but about happiness and unhappiness" in life. He said that becoming entangled in concerns over matters such as profits (revenues or income) turns you into a slave because in so doing you lose control over your inner world. To Epictetus the true meaning of success in life did not involve profits.

Just as with Confucius and Mencius, Epictetus felt that ethics rather than profits, power or status should be the main focus of human striving. He taught that human beings should concern themselves with pursuing mental peace and you attained this by learning how to free yourself from being controlled by your thoughts. He taught the Stoic view that "virtue is sufficient for happiness."

Just as we learned in the story of Liao Fan, the Stoic Epictetus taught

"The course of the Will determines good or bad fortune, and one's balance of misery and happiness." In Stoic philosophy, a man needs to master his willpower to do good and refrain from evil, to ennoble his behavior, and refrain from succumbing to what is lower. The Confucian way emphasizes that we master our thoughts, attitudes, emotions, willpower and the changes of phenomena, and the Stoic way of Epictetus also speaks of the same mission. The Stoics believed that we shouldn't let our emotions result in errors of judgment, and that we should work with others and treat everyone in a fair and just manner. In Stoicism all people were considered manifestations of the one universal spirit (which has parallels to the Supreme Ultimate of Confucianism) and should therefore live in brotherly love helping one another.

The reason we have made a sidetrack to Epictetus is because his teachings on how we should handle the mind are similar to ACT, so now we have three schools of thought intersecting with the same conclusions and guidance. In general, the Stoics held that one could transform emotions by developing clear judgment (wisdom) and inner calm, which is the Confucian way in another form. A man, through dispassion (detachment) could also learn how to become indifferent to pain, pleasure, joy or grief just as happens naturally with correct mindfulness practice.

Epictetus taught that for all men there are (a) things within your power that are therefore "up to you," and (b) things beyond your power or "not up to you." Stoics are taught to work on *what they have control over* and to be accepting, or indifferent, to what they cannot control. To have concern over what you cannot control brings you no benefit since there is nothing you can do about it. Thus a Stoic is taught to discipline his mind in the same way as ACT. He relies on virtue, reason, self-control and mental fortitude as a means of overcoming the control of destructive emotions. The only thing that ultimately compels you, claimed Epictetus, should not be your thoughts or emotions but your will. In short, how you apply your will is what matters in life.

If you covet things beyond your power and control such as externals like fame or fortune (things controlled by others who may or may not give them to you), you actually become a slave to emotions such as desire, fear or anxiety. Epictetus said, "A man's master is he who is able to confer or remove whatever that man seeks or shuns. Whoever then would be free, let him wish nothing, let him decline nothing, which depends on others; else he must necessarily be a slave."

James Bond Stockdale, who became a prisoner of war who underwent eight years of regular torture, wrote *Courage Under Fire* recounting his ordeal. A student of Epictetus, whose philosophy mentally saved him, Stockdale refused to desire things from his torturers. As an incredibly valuable lesson for us all, Stockdale explained that if you want to remain ultimately free then you should not seek from others what they control and you do not, but must remain indifferent to the fate of their giving or taking things away. He explained that to remain fully human and retain your inner respect in times of torture and difficulty you must learn detachment from the contents of your mind. You must teach yourself to become indifferent to whatever you cannot control. In other words, if there are "changes" you cannot master or manipulate, then because you cannot do anything about them you should resign yourself to their outcomes.

Your will and actions are the only thing you can control in life. What should therefore occupy your concern is your actions and behavior controlled by your will, namely how to behave in the world under all types of circumstances. You cannot always control the outcome of your behavior but you can always try to go beyond yourself by making it the best possible, expressive of your highest values, and move forward from there.

For example, while an exemplary man should try to build a good reputation through positive behavior, other people are the ones who actually decide your reputation. You should therefore focus only on acting in a virtuous manner, since this is what builds a reputation, rather than run after a reputation. Whether it comes or not is a matter of fate. Otherwise you will become like the vaporous movie stars and singers who pursue fame as if it were profit, often doing the unmentionable to win an empty prize. Commenting on people who pursue a reputation, Epictetus said that your reputation is not something to get mixed up with your moral purpose.

Epictetus taught the importance of cultivating the supremacy of your mind and willpower saying, "It is neither death, nor exile, nor toil, nor any such things that is the cause of your doing, or not doing, anything, but only your opinions and the decisions of your Will." Just as ACT teaches, our mind controls our actions and behavior; to control our behavior we must therefore learn to control our mind, and ultimately our will.

What you think ultimately decides what you do in life and what you do determines what you achieve. To a Stoic, self-cultivation is therefore ultimately about how you discipline your mind to control your actions and behavior to attain accomplishment or serenity, which parallels the Confucian way. Because of such viewpoints, if you wish to study the way of Confucian cultivation you would surely benefit from also studying Stoicism as well. Stoicism also teaches that the mind is a tool that must be mastered.

The Confucian way is that we should only take actions in line with our highest values, and must always return to our values no matter how often we go off track. Confucius and Mencius also both said that our values should never be based on seeking profit, which the Stoics taught as well. Our values should revolve around morality and ethics, relationships, virtuous living, and with cultivating the Way.

In all of this, please remember that the cultivation way eschews profits over people. For instance, at one time Confucius's stables were burnt down while he was away. The first question that a rich man would normally ask upon returning would be if any of his expensive prize horses were hurt, but Confucius immediately asked, "Were any people injured?" This shows his emphasis on humanity rather than wealth and possessions. He did not treat humans as commodities.

Confucius is important because he takes us out of egotism and materialism to altruism. He provided many examples of proper behavior like this, providing us with valuable lessons on the template for proper behavior. His *Analects* should therefore be considered a lifetime teaching text for ourselves, our communities and our world.

At the beginning of this chapter we were eavesdropping on a conversation between Mencius and King Hui of Liang that went as follows:

> Why must Your Majesty speak of "profit"? Let there simply be benevolence and righteousness. If your majesty says, "How can I profit my state?" the Chief Counselors will say, "How can I profit my clan?" and the nobles and commoners will say, "How can I profit my self?" Superiors and subordinates will seize profit from each other, and the state will be endangered. ... Never have the benevolent left their parents behind. Never have the righteous put their ruler last. Let Your Majesty speak only of benevolence and righteousness. Why must one speak of "profit"?

The famous Confucian philosopher Huang Zongxi once wrote, "A real man does what is right regardless of his self-interest; does what is sensible regardless of success or failure; and does what is good for future generations, not just for his own generation." When someone obtains a career, job or occupation the Confucian way is to keep these principles in mind.

Consider the following. We belong to the realm of animals but have, through the use of our minds, gradually risen above them through the creation of culture, civilization and society. However, it is a constant battle not to give in to our animal nature. If we were to let ourselves to be guided in life by the pursuit of self-interest and profits alone, like a Ferengi on Star Trek, what actions would not be forbidden in the pursuit of profits? For instance, if the purpose of life was purely self-interest then why should we be honest? Why not just steal with cleverness so that you escape being caught since honesty will severely limit your wealth? How are we not like animals if we act in this manner? Furthermore, how can we extend this realization to corporations that pursue profitability to such an extent that they actually harm humanity?

As oxygen is important for life but is not the point of life, profitability is necessary for a business to survive but should not be considered the purpose of the business. You must think of it this way: a business has a purpose of adding value or benefit and profit is the measuring stick of that addition. Profit is necessary for a firm's survival, but if you want the owners and employees to consider it as having a higher purpose then profit should be viewed as the payment for adding value, benefit and welfare to peoples' lives.

Profit enables a business to continue providing a *service mission* to others that supplies benefit or value, and so it is necessary for survival just as is the capitalist system if people want protection of their personal assets. Leftists tend to push for collectivist solutions to problems (where individuals are considered disposable while the group is supreme) such as Communism, Bolshevism, Marxism or Leninism-Trotskyism but those systems are based on phantasmagorical delusions. They have been historically revealed everywhere as utter failures. Their only result has been unimaginable human suffering and the dehumanization of entire populations while leadership elites enjoy the benefits of power.

Men become powerless to live with dignity when such systems rule. In a practical sense time and again they ultimately boil down to the idea that citizens only exist to serve the state. They lead to people living their entire lives under a virtual slavery of thought, word and deed trying to meet the demands of those in control. The only realism ever produced by such –isms has been death, terror and suffering.

No economic system is perfect, but for all its faults the capitalist system is still the best, especially when certain protections are rendered for the population that temper its potential abuses. As Max Weber analyzed matters, the rise of capitalism is actually due to the values of Protestantism, and clearly illustrates Confucius's views that cultural values are what promote civilization.

Capitalism, which espouses the self-determination of the individual, allows men and women to make a fundamental contribution to society of their own choosing. It allows for the evolution of the self to be put at the forefront of society. Even so the pursuit of private interests, however essential to progress and human flourishing, should not be allowed to destructively infringe upon the public good. There must be legal restraints against massive abuse. Businesses must certainly be economically self-sustaining but not infringe upon people and the public purpose.

While the profit motive can be socially destructive if left unchecked, capitalism allows social energies to be concentrated upon the promotion of economic means that carry the promise of social improvement, thus serving a social end. Under capitalism, which makes human strength productive, personal strengths create social benefits. The profit motive prized by capitalism is not and never should be the supreme ruler of social behavior, but of all systems available the capitalist free market is best of all. Fascism is a disaster and the problem with socialism, as attractive as it seems to intellectuals, is that socialist governments soon run out of "other people's money" for their missions.

I want you to think of matters this way. Both Buddhism and Hinduism arose in India where human beings surveyed the sad fact that life is difficult, full of suffering, and in nature all around animals are cruelly killing one another for food. Animals experience a constant fear of death because they are always in danger of being eaten or not finding food. Everyone is a prey and predator, for even a deer is a predator to the grass. Every victim in nature is also somehow a victimizer and there is no escape from this painful, burdensome cycle of life.

Humans would act just like animals and engage in unrestrained killing, thieving and raping if cultural constraints were not imposed upon their behavior. Men will even kill one another just because of different ideas in their heads and have done so continually throughout history. Nonetheless, humans are also capable of higher thoughts and conceptions that enable them to rise above their animal nature. This is because man can invent civilization and culture. Culture and civilization have tamed a large measure of man's barbarity and wildness.

Through purifying thought, discipline and self-cultivation man becomes capable of an ennoblement that transcends the ordinary realm of the animals. He can rise above the animalistic role play of predators and prey such as a stronger stealing the possessions of the weaker. The continual striving to uplift yourself above this sort of behavior is the entire purpose of Confucian cultivation. While it is not religion, it is a spiritual path of purification when you choose to use its methods!

On the one side stands nature where there is a web of eaters and the eaten. On the other side there are humans who can create civilization and culture where the laws of the jungle are transcended; human behavior can elevate itself above naked self-interest such as motivations of sex, power. money and preeminence. This is what Confucius wants everyone to strive for. This is the meaning of consummate conduct. The Confucian way is to pursue consummate conduct, benevolence, ennoblement, or exemplary behavior rather than simply pursue profits, which is akin to the realm of the animals once again.

Pursuing a higher purpose is the main thing that separates man from the animals. It is what produces a meaningful life, and it is a life of strong values and higher purpose that we must take as our ideal. We are all citizens of a country owing allegiance to it, members of communities with responsibilities within it, members of families with relationship duties to our parents, spouses and children, and friends to others. These are all relationships that need to be cultivated. Each of us have identities within these frameworks (national, civic, community, familial, friendship, religious, etc.) and what we do within these relationships *by being led by our rational minds* is what gives our lives meaning.

Everyone wants to live a meaningful life with purpose, but how do you do that? How do you give yourself a purpose so that you can bear the inevitable suffering that life entails? How do you protect yourself from living an unfulfilling miserable script that only pursues what is necessary for survival? To do so you need direction as to a higher life purpose and that direction must come from your own values.

You have to separate yourself from the script you are presently following and ask, "Who am I? What do I stand for? What do I ultimately want to do in life? What do I want to accomplish? What do I want to make of myself? How do I want to be in whatever I must do? Despite my circumstances, am I living my ideal of an honorable and virtuous life? Am I living in good faith to my true values? Am I cultivating my humanity? Am I committed to my own individual excellence? Am I living life for work or for being a human being? Am I a person creating benefit for others? Am I doing anything that society finds useful? Am I helping to make a better future? Are my goals serving a higher purpose? Am I trying to make a difference, do as well as I possibly can or do things better than they have ever been done before? At the end of my life, facing death, will I be able to say that it is better that I was here? Did I remain silent, or did I stand up and raise my voice?"

You are the one who has to answer such questions and find a sense of purpose within life, for no one can or will do it for you. Meaning is a form of personal vision that lets you know it is all worthwhile. In order to fully embody the self-determination of personal meaning and purpose you must draw guidance from deeper spiritual values inside you. Then you must live according to those values in order to experience a life worth living. There are many goals and purposes you can choose for your life or within your life, but all the roads of meaning, purpose, satisfaction and contentment will entail that you become a better moral person.

You can never know whether you will rise enough in life to become great in terms of wealth, power, fame, status or some other prestige. You cannot even know whether you will achieve the goals you want either. You don't know whether you will even be living tomorrow. The future isn't under your control but your will is, and thus so is your behavior. What is under your control is your ability to move ahead in life in accordance with your values and getting back on track whenever you wander.

Unfortunately, most people are limited in their ability to do the things they want in life because they are constricted by the circumstances in which they live. For instance, because of the economy you might not be lucky enough to obtain a satisfying job to put bread on the table and might not have enough free time either. However, no matter how scanty the resources you have any voluntary activities you undertake (exercise, reading, meditation, singing, learning a new skill, etc.) can provide you with a way to exercise your values.

You might not be able to achieve any of your big goals in life, but you can remain committed to your values and work on perfecting your behavior no matter how long or short or wholesome or poor your life might be. People normally feel there is no such thing as a good life during a state of want, but as much as you suffer during deprivation you are always left with your ethics and values.

Everyone in life is actually always seeking how to get out of a state of misery and move into a happier state. When pursing excitement, distraction or material indulgences, most people don't realize that they are actually seeking serenity - a more peaceful place in their life. Everyone is also seeking a road to exhibit their integrity and authenticity. We are all seeking a way to present ourselves to the world as the core of who we really are. To do so we must break the negative habit energies that hide our true selves so that we always appear straightforward and authentic.

Thoughts can guide us and thoughts can hamper us in this quest. They are just experiences in your head and nothing more. Sometimes they are even a barrier that doesn't let you directly experience your surroundings clearly because your mind layers on too many emotional memories and preconceptions. Confucian mindfulness unhooks us from this and thus brings us back to the world of direct experience and authenticity. Aren't you after this? This is the Confucian way.

Previously we examined Frank McKinney's method of reviewing his life on a regular basis in order to strike a balance between profit-seeking and purpose. In order to provide his business with a higher mission other than just making money, once a year he would set aside some time to review his business and try to see it from a higher perspective. During that annual event he would go through an exercise to hammer out a core ideology of purpose and values that embodied a higher service mission other than just profits. Then he sought some way to align his goals, strategies, and actions around that higher mission that he had just refreshed for his own benefit.

In *Make It Big! 49 Secrets for Building a Life of Extreme Success* he wrote, "This simple planning process—setting aside one weekend a year to create a new personal vision statement, and then taking a couple of hours each

Saturday to establish the goals that will help me turn that vision into reality—has been the bedrock underlying my success for the past 10 years. Once I started doing this, I found a marked change in my life and in my results. Sure, I was accomplishing more, since I was taking the time to plan my week. But more than that, I was linking my weekly goals to the vision of who I wanted to be.

"A personal vision and mission statement is the agreement you make with yourself that this is who you want to be, how you want to act, what you will and won't do, and how you want to appear in the world. It's also a living, breathing document that will change over the years. I know there are some people who like to create 5- and 10-year plans for their lives, but I'm not one of them. Sure, I can have a sense of who I want to be 10 years from now, but I have found that redoing my vision every year keeps it fresh. It allows me to take into account the progress I have or haven't made and set my direction based on what I see as my next step. After all, I have the big picture of my highest calling … that pulls me toward my ultimate future much more strongly than a 5- or 10-year plan. …"

Creating a mission or vision statement for a business or career is taking one of the first important steps of aligning yourself with a higher calling that you can be proud of in life. Turning that service mission into tangible operational goals is then the next step to take. Do your quarterly or yearly goals have anything to do with your larger mission or are they just about money? This is something McKinney would always ask himself.

Continuing he explained, "The last step is to make sure your daily efforts represent the goals you've set and the vision you've created. When your business spends its days pursuing goals based on your corporate vision, your customers as well as the business community will see you as having integrity. And isn't that the kind of reputation you want?"[12]

Frank McKinney's writings reveals a clear understanding that business must be profitable, but your business can also encompass a higher purpose other than just the quest for profitability. He personally started viewing his business as improving the state of the world. He saw its purpose as offering benefit, value and service to others. Can you do this, and even rearrange your business to perform more of this function?

It is definitely proper to view your business from the aspect of a larger

---

[12] Frank McKinney, *Make It Big! 49 Secrets for Building a Life of Extreme Success* (John Wiley & Sons, New York, 2002), pp. 27-28, 30.

mission such as that you are building a cathedral rather than simply building a wall or that your business is meant to help humanity. This type of thinking will help you align your actions with a higher outcome. You cannot dispense with the need for profits but the proper ideal to maintain ethical behavior while pursuing profits and a mission of service is the Confucian way.

As we have seen over and over again, it is of great benefit to step back on a daily, weekly, quarterly and even yearly basis and ask yourself, "Is my life on track? What do I want my life to be about? Where are my actions taking me? Am I growing in the right direction? Are the goals I am seeking worthy of my time and effort? Is my behavior reflecting my values? What is the ultimate purpose of my career or business other than just making money? Am I living with integrity?" For true personal success and happiness in life, one's personal goals and caring goals must synchronize.

The great management expert Peter Drucker once said, "Always ask yourself if you are doing the right thing before doing things right." Ask first if you are doing the right, correct thing! We must all follow our own moral compass in life, which is part of the Great Learning, but if your moral sense is broken you can create a living hell for yourself and others.

The Confucian way is to always practice mindfulness, but also to give pause for reflection and ponder such things on a regular basis. You should do this while always pursuing the path of consummate conduct and holding to an intent to make a positive contribution to society.

The methods you have been taught will enable you to do this in many ways. They will help you deal with thoughts as objects rather than realities. They give you a structure for understanding how personal change happens starting with the mind, and can help you change your attitudes, habit energies and behavior. They can help you to decide the purpose of your life and ultimate direction you want to take with your actions. You can develop a purpose *for* life and *within* life as a result of these methods.

The Great Learning in life is learning how to use our minds to control our attitudes and behavior and direct our lives in wholesome, valuable directions. The Confucian way teaches you just this. It helps you make significant fundamental changes to get to where you want to go.

CHAPTER 11:
YOUR LIFE PURPOSE AND
PURPOSES WITHIN YOUR LIFE

The Confucian Zhang Zai said that the ideal purpose or goal of life entails:

To establish true mind for the universe,
To build up a good life for the populace,
To re-establish the discontinued studies of the ancient sages, and
To establish great peace for 10,000 generations.

Master Nan Huai Chin always said that one's life purpose should include the following three objectives: "realizing enlightenment, saving people and saving the world." Since most people would not consider this their life purpose, you should consider these objectives as possible *purposes within life* that you might work to accomplish.

Too often people are looking for one greater life purpose and become befuddled and bewildered when they actually should be devoted to a number of smaller purposes within life that they feel are important. You must decide whether to be pursuing a vision of establishing virtue, justice, prosperity or anything else for others and then work toward it. One guiding principle is that a purpose is more motivating if it is bigger than yourself.

"Saving the people," which Confucius called "loving the people," doesn't mean that you must undertake grandiose actions or missions. It simply means that you should try to contribute as much as you can. Most people don't have big resources and not everyone can be a superman of compassion with a superhuman commitment like Albert Schweitzer who donated his life to help others. While the work of Mahatma Gandhi, Mother Theresa, Muhammad Yunus, or Martin Luther King can be incredibly inspiring, few can emulate the great sacrifices they made. Few of us can consider such great missions, especially when we know that such roads are filled with deprivation and hardship. The ideal is to definitely help make the world a better place as much as you can even though your contribution might be small. Small does not matter. It means cooperating with others in all sorts of ways to help to bring peace and prosperity to the world.

What people are really seeking in life is some way to make a contribution, some way to be part of a larger context or mission. People want to feel that their life has meaning, and they usually feel that it does when it incorporates service to and care for others. Life has meaning when it is not an ascetic's solitude but involves an active virtuous participation in a larger whole.

All people, whether they know it or not, are seeking to forget themselves and bring their lives into harmony with something they deem divine, transcendental or universal – a larger and more perfect greatness. They are seeking a connection between their own lives and a larger context outside of it. That larger context is the condition of your community, society, nation, and world. The context is the fact, previously discussed, that you are intimately bound up with everyone such that the burdens and benefits of others are also yours through the interdependence of cause and effect. Therefore by alleviating the pains and sufferings of others/society you not just help them but yourself.

There is a pervasiveness of suffering in the world, but if everyone acts just a tiny bit altruistically so as to improve the whole, do not we all benefit from a better whole that becomes elevated because its burdens have been reduced? Do we not all share in that benefit, including the giver? Isn't this the way to materialize the dream of a better society? It doesn't need grand schemes. It just needs the multitude of many tiny beneficial actions.

We have an opportunity to make a difference rather than simply be mechanical cogs within a wheel. Our lives are actually valuable because in this universe we are the rare phenomena that have consciousness so that we can think and act in ways to make things better.

Associating With Larger Groups

Although most of us can only make a small contribution in helpful directions, nonetheless many great men have taken upon themselves lofty goals of not just helping themselves and their families but of extending a helpful influence to their community, state and then the world. As Confucius said in *The Great Learning*, one extends their influence outwards from themselves to their family, their community, and then larger groups of men. This is the standard progression of expansion, which is to progressively enlarge one's group feelings to greater wholes starting from identification with your family to your clan, society, state, country and world.

Napoleon Hill taught us how to extend our influence and associations to a larger group and use it to help our own selves using a Mastermind alliance. In a Mastermind alliance a group of men come together for similar interests. A common focus brings the people together to solve problems and work on some common goals. They pool their mind-power, experience, education and knowledge and move in response to a common motive to change things for the better.

Can a small group of people actually change the world or a community even though small? Margaret Mead correctly said, "Never doubt that a small group of thoughtful, committed citizens can change the world; indeed it's the only thing that ever has." Local level initiatives can produce national and international fruits.

The Mastermind alliance has been used across the world to achieve all sorts of objectives, and is something you should start using. There are many such useful techniques in Napoleon's Hill's success classic *Think and Grow Rich*, which has sold over 100 million copies since it was initially written to become one of the most popular self-improvement classics of all time. I urge you to read it; most business millionaires have.

If you start banding together with a group of people of like mind then camaraderie will sustain you during your efforts to achieve group objectives. Even Benjamin Franklin formed a Mastermind group, creating a mutual improvement club in Philadelphia named the Junto whose club members met on a weekly basis to encourage each other's intellectual pursuits. You should use participation in a group like this to achieve your greater objectives.

All progress in the world starts with an individual, and that individual might even be *you* for some special initiative. Some unexpected spark of motivation might suddenly turn you into a hero of change. All one can say is that change in the world starts with awareness, action and a commitment to perseverance of effort. It starts with what you think, say and do and moves on to how this involves others. It involves learning how to use your mind rightly to accomplish what you want. Thus the importance of the Confucian way for mastering your mind.

From the work on ennobling your personal conduct you can influence your family, community and then the larger world for the better. You are almost always influencing others in some way even if you don't know it. You can also band together with others of like rapport to pursue some mission of higher calling that serves a greater objective. After all, many people want to add something to life and this is a way to do it.

Confucius made it perfectly clear that self-cultivation ("learning") involved cultivating a heart of public virtue, which we can also call beneficial cooperation or altruism. Buddhism calls this charity or compassion while Christianity calls this "good works." The purpose of self-cultivation is not withdrawal from the world, but rather an altruistic active participation in the world dependent on contemplative reasoning. Think before and while you act. It is a commitment to positive change through personal efforts. In *Analects* 2.2 Confucius said, "The three hundred items in the *Book of Songs* (a foundational text of Chinese culture) can be concentrated into a single expression: Charge forth without swerving."

According to Confucius, personal conduct is always tied to social action; you cultivate yourself in order to be a helpful actor to people. The Confucian way thus mirrors the ideals of Christianity to make the world a little better because you are in it. As Zengzi had said (*Analects* 4.15), "The Master's way lies in exerting all one's effort (giving one's utmost) and relating to the needs of others."

According to Confucius, you don't have to be a hero who stands apart from others, but you should strive to better your own behavior and become a positive influence on others. The best way to influence others is to first become a model of behavior yourself by deciding to devote yourself to consummate conduct. This is the road that Benjamin Franklin chose.

The spiritual path doesn't start with rabble-rousing that demands a better government or utopian world, but starts with this decision to perfect your own individual behavior instead. You must be unrelentingly persistent in trying to cultivate a higher standard of personal behavior using the transformative process of self-correction, which is why the Confucian way espouses mindful self-observation. First change yourself, and then "guide the changes" to help others.

Cultivating consummate conduct (man being his very best) was the center of all Confucius's teachings and should become the center of your life today, the center of your life story. Since we cannot control what arises as our thoughts nor control the results of our actions, and since we cannot even control our fate then is this not what life is about? Is it not about learning how to use our mind as a tool, and learning how to properly deal with our thoughts and will? Is it not about the path of behavioral ennoblement? Whether there is an afterlife or not, we can and should consider this life a process of purification.

As your own behavior improves from the admirable self-effort to become better than how you currently are, your conduct can serve as a model that radiates the message of proper conduct to others. Confucius stated in *Analects* 12.17, "The key to governing lies in being correct. When leaders are themselves correct their influence will pervade the rest of society." The more that you perfect your behavior towards ennoblement, the greater can and will be your influence in the outer world. The message is to go ahead and try to be the possible person you always wanted.

Thoughts are needed to guide our cultivation of self-control and ennoblement, and yet thoughts are also our problem. However, one of the most powerful principles discovered by modern research is that thinking lofty thoughts can help us achieve control of our thoughts, just as Confucius recommended. Lofty thoughts, such as devoting yourself to something larger than yourself, can guide you away from lower actions and the baser habits of behavior that are leftovers from the barbaric realm of animals.

Lofty thoughts and goals raise us higher. Giving in to baser thoughts and instincts takes us lower. Think in high-level terms to inspire yourself, associate with others similarly motivated whenever possible, and this will help guide your behavior to something better, which is the Confucian way. We must all cultivate lofty goals in life and a persevering spirit to try to reach them.

The methods of Confucian cultivation are so powerful because they are clean, non-denominational and extremely effective at helping people attain their higher goals in life. They can separate you from your animal nature so that you are not ruled by the irrational mind. By emphasizing the rational mind together with mental discipline they lead to an ennoblement stage of existence - they spiritualize the individual. They also purify and harmonize society. The road of spirituality simply involves a process of learning how to use the qualities of your mind to become a true human being rather than a beast.

Whether we employ the related methods of Liao Fan, Benjamin Franklin, Frank Bettger, Napoleon Hill, Frank McKinney and others, rest assured that the method of mindfulness when practiced with persevering, resilient commitment will change your life for the better. They will enable you to overcome the environmental and even astrological influences of fate. When you can so purify yourself that you always rise above these normally dominant influences then you will have become a master, a man who can skillfully operate and control his mind. This is the objective of a sage. At this point you can become a great leader of mankind.

Mindfulness exercises our mental muscles to observe our behavior and its impact on others. It teaches us to distinguish between good and evil in real time so that we can do more of one and less of another. The Confucian way of mindfulness in its various forms has enabled countless people to raise themselves higher by purifying their behavior so that they could accomplish great things. Although only a small minority might subscribe to its standards, everywhere it produces the best. When we ask how "good behavior" may best be developed in society, the method is by promoting the non-denominational methods of the Confucian way. A man is to master his mind not only to accomplish great things in the world, but also so as to beautify his behavior and find the greatest internal peace and happiness.

The structured method of Liao Fan/Franklin, if you truly apply it to your daily life with consistency, will radically transform all your outcomes just as it did for Franklin and Liao Fan. The baseball player Frank Bettger, wishing to change his business fortunes, reasoned that it should also work for him in the business field via his sales efforts. It paid off in spades, which he recounted in *How I Raised Myself From Failure to Success in Selling*. Dale Carnegie and Frank McKinney revealed how to successfully use it on larger time scales to have even greater impacts on your life purpose. These are all sample methods you should emulate.

Death can snatch us at a moment's notice, so knowing this you must ask yourself what goals, purposes or objectives are truly worthy of your life. What holds meaning since you can die at any moment due to some unforeseen accident? Confucius advised (*Analects* 4.8), "If at dawn one hears and grasps the Way, even death can be faced at dusk." Know the path and get started – this is enough.

Determining a life purpose is truly a subjective thing. It is something *you* create because you define it yourself. Yours is different than mine, and it should be that way because no two people are alike. You can derive inspiration from others for developing your own life purpose, but it should truly be yours alone. Some purposes can be large and some should be humble because the resources and circumstances available to you prevent a greater vision from being possible. Who can criticize you as to whether you go for something big or stay with something small? At the end of your life, you are the final judge who measures yourself. The key determinant to success or not is whether your efforts have helped care for other people, meaning that what you did mattered to people other than yourself. This is what gives a life purpose true meaning other than its existence as simply a goal.

In any form that it takes, Confucian practices should be part of the personal effort you make to fulfill your life purposes. Whatever you choose to accomplish in life – be it a somewhat minor goal or a higher, loftier objective – the going will be easier when you use the methods of Confucian cultivation. I have detailed the best methods in *Quick, Fast, Done* and *Move Forward* to help with your journey.

Wherever you apply your efforts in life there will be a result. What will that result be? Not a single human being can guarantee your success in achieving your dreams or goals, but you can certainly maximize your chances of doing that. Confucian cultivation provides a reliable vehicle and structural guide to help you get there. The only question is what pursuits are worthy of your time.

Your life has a time limit, and if you do not use your time wisely then you will not have a second opportunity for each second lost. If we have an opportunity to benefit the world and then don't use it, when will it come again? Since our moments of life are limited, valuing the moments we have means they should be put to good use. That being the case, what will you fill your life with in the free moments still left to you?

Charity and Merit Making

Here we should once again turn to the topic of merit because life purpose is ultimately about the creation of merit from trying to build a better world. Liao Fan and his master both taught that accumulating merit is necessary if we want to be able to change our fortunes for the better. Confucius also taught that the purpose of self-improvement was social engagement in moral acts of service to the community, which is creating merit. Ben Franklin, through a wide variety of his actions, also showed a dedication to altruistically helping people through many acts of charitable merit. Because few understand what "merit" entails or how to accumulate it, let us reveal some of the practical ways by which we can improve our lives and those of others by performing merit.

The question is, what are the various types of good deeds we can do in life that might produce for us a stock of merit? Buddhism, for instance, traditionally says there are three forms of charity that accumulate merit: giving money and material goods, giving helpful teachings or instructions (*dharma*) to others, and giving them fearlessness (confidence or mental support). If we decided to devote ourselves to performing such good deeds in order to collect their positive results as "merit," what should those deeds then be? What did Liao Fan, for instance, devote himself to?

Liao Fan showed through his confession it was his own faults – what he called his own lack of virtue - that prevented him from achieving the merit he desired in life such as obtaining a son and higher position. He started to accumulate merit by not only doing good deeds but by transforming his own attitudes and behavior.

When you are virtuous, moral and righteous in your behavior you are accumulating merit, and Confucius emphasized that this was more important than pursuing profits, status, power or any other objective in life. Basically, when you extend kindness and respect to others in ways such as charity, without doing so as a calculated investment seeking a dividend, this is accumulating merit.

Most people lack the wealth of independent means so they must work for a living. Holding a job is their primary source of income and they usually do not have much money to spare. Some people, however, start businesses to create income. One way to help these people and generate merit might be by offering them practical support for their business or occupation such as farming. This could be done by extending resources to them or even by offering courses on success training.

A perfect example of such help might be to support Kiva.org, which makes microloans to budding entrepreneurs so that they can create micro-businesses that improve their lives. Heifer International also makes the gift of farm animals to those in poverty while teaching the recipients how to raise them. The animals will typically produce both food and income for poor families for the rest of their lives. When an animal reproduces, the gift recipient is charged with the responsibility of also making a similar gift to others.

Another way to help others is by supporting those who are suffering disabilities such as those who are blind, deaf, or disabled. Many charitable organizations have been established to do just this, and focus on helping those who are suffering through a variety of different means. By supporting these charities with your labor or funds you also build merit.

When we find people who are mentally suffering in life and teach them the way to happiness, such as teaching them the methods of Confucian cultivation or that taking niacin supplements can end mental illness, we also generate merit. Once we help people recognize that happiness or unhappiness comes from within their own minds then we can help them cut off their unhappiness and create new mental attitudes.

Sometimes we cannot stop the mental pain a person experiences. However, we might be able to help reduce their pain and prevent those individuals from doing whatever might create future pain and misery. In ministering to others this way, even though we might stand at a higher vantage point we still need to accord with their dispositions. Skillfulness and patience are required in yourself if you want to help others and prevent them from pursuing goals that work against their own happiness. Nonetheless, the overall principle is that directing those heading for trouble back to the right path is a type of merit. This type of service improves peoples' lives by helping them avoid present and future suffering.

Another means of helping others, which is espoused by most religions across the world, is to extend courtesy to travelers and assist them in a gracious and friendly way. In many cultures it has always been considered of great merit to offer hospitality - including food, medicine or accommodations - to strangers on journeys. As John Wesley's maxim summarized, you try to: "Do all the good you can, by all the means you can, in all the ways you can, in all the places you can, at all the times you can, to all the people you can, as long as ever you can."

Another means of aiding others is by "offering fearlessness," which means protecting, calming or giving confidence to people who are unsettled because of suffering anxiety or fear. For instance, we might console the grief-stricken who lose their possessions due to some tragedy or suffer the loss of loved ones. This is offering fearlessness. By offering counseling, resources, and other types of support to those at emotional lows we can accumulate merit by lightening their load and helping them recover. By helping the emotionally discouraged we can assist them to get over troubles and continue onwards in the pursuit of a higher purpose.

Another type of merit-making is protecting life. For instance, helping people survive an accident, paying for a surgical operation or medicine, or protecting people from discovery during times of persecution is a type of merit-making. Volunteers who try to save animals from being burned in forest fires, dying from toxic oil spills, or from being cruelly farmed and killed also accumulate this type of merit. Becoming vegetarian or reducing your meat intake also falls into this category of merit-making as does protecting people's jobs since protecting their income preserves their lives.

While we might not be able to free people from prison, including those jailed unjustly, we can often help those in prison in order to accumulate merit. We can also provide aid to those suffering torture or refused basic human rights by contributing to organizations like Amnesty International that champion human rights and freedom.

Helping the poor and needy through charity is another way to accumulate merit. This type of merit-making is called "giving wealth" and means addressing poverty with various remedies that involve sharing what we have. "Giving wealth" doesn't just mean giving money to the needy but providing valuable resources they might need to improve their conditions. For example, you might provide the needy with some of the basic necessities for life they need but are too poor to purchase. We can even help finance special events in their life such as by paying for funeral costs or wedding expenses as is done in Chinese culture.

Charitable contributions always generate merit but when people have little income, how is giving charity possible? Remember that charity is not just giving money. It is a type of sacrificing of yourself for the sake of others, either for individuals or for a collective good. It is sacrificing your individual advantages (whether they be money, time, labor, etc.) for the sake of someone else's benefit in order to help them.

You should also consider charity as a type of *cooperation*. Civic participation (which societies hope to encourage by stressing the ideal of "civic duty") is a form of charity, or we can say that charity is a form of civic participation since it helps others. Charity, whether provided by individuals or a group, is basically a form of cooperation.

Cooperation is the glue that holds societies together. Religion usually provides the integrative ideology that helps hold society together because it engenders cooperation at a very large scale beyond ethnic communities. Religion serves an integrative role for society by instilling cooperation among disparate groups. This is important for a nation, which is why groups trying to take over a country immediately try to fracture religion.

Charity itself, in terms of helping others, must be seen in the same way as it is also a form of beneficial public cooperation that helps glue people together. It is a cooperative contribution to others - a means of providing some form of aid or goods that benefit members of society.

Without having income to spare, one's time and labor volunteered for the public welfare (doing something for others instead of leisure) are indeed a form of charity that you can also label as beneficial cooperation for the good of all. The contribution, in whatever form it takes, is a kind of sacrifice for the welfare of others. By engaging in charity you help others, and when many more people act benevolently in the same way then everyone will benefit from this cooperative effort. Cooperation or harmony builds societies, which is one of the reasons that it is stressed in the Confucian way.

Cooperation is not just one of the things that societies do - *it is the main thing they do*, so it must be encouraged in all ways possible. Without mutual trust and cooperation between its members most societies will collapse into instability and disorder. The byproduct will be social dysfunction. Without the cooperation of the masses, sometimes a ruling government is overthrown through revolution too. Confucius often taught lessons on how to rule a country by stressing social harmony, which is why I am emphasizing these lessons that update his original teachings.

Societies are built upon the foundation of cooperation, which includes altruistic acts of charity that solve problems for the public good. When you examine many historical events such as the collapse of the Roman Empire, the Hundred Years War, English Civil War, the Russian Revolution and War of the Roses you will find that disintegrating cooperation was a leading indicator of the coming social collapse.

Countries disintegrate when they lose their ability to cooperate at the level of the whole society, which is why public holidays, ceremonies and shared national ideals are needed to keep strong the glue of social cohesion. Failed states, more often than not, suffer from losing their ability to cooperate at the level of the entire society. This is why charity, in sacrificing for others' benefit, helps build communities and national solidarity. The very fact that many members in a society think of others in this way reveals a strong degree of cooperative spirit in the country, making it harder to conquer, and that common attitude will also help those people to achieve any shared goals.

Addressing spiritual poverty is another means of rendering assistance to others and thereby accumulating merit. Many people have a strong longing to seek inner change or outer behavioral change but don't know how to bring it about. Seeking personal change is usually a do-it-yourself project but people often have no one to turn to for guidance and advice. By teaching others the road of genuine spiritual practice, which includes meditation and reflective self-correction, we can help them to positively change their lives.

True spiritual training teaches people how to properly deal with their thoughts, how to counteract disturbing emotions and afflictions, how to master many life skills, and how to transform themselves through self-correction. Devoting yourself to the Way will change your life for the better. The far-reaching positive effects of the Confucian way cannot be understated.

Since Buddhism says we should "do good, avoid evil, never oppose all unborn good from being born but oppose all evil from being born," accumulating merit means supporting others involved in various types of good works and helping them in their efforts. Benjamin Franklin, for instance, led a large number of private, voluntary initiatives to enhance society during his life. Though a Deist, he financially contributed to nearly every church in Philadelphia, including the first synagogue, since he felt that houses of worship helped people fortify their self-discipline and morality.

He was non-denominational in his outlook.

A final type of merit-making is to remind people who practice charity of the excellent results they have brought about due to their efforts, which in turn encourages givers to continue their social contributions. Everyone likes to hear they did a good job or good deed, and publicly recognizing whoever gives is a form of merit that encourages equivalent efforts from others in society. As a form of merit we can also work to remove obstacles standing in the way of people trying to do these good deeds and encourage/support them so they are not discouraged in their attempts. We want to see more of such offerings rather than less.

The Time Remaining

Since the crux of any life purpose or purposes within life involve improving yourself and helping to build a better world, ask yourself what merit you want to do with the time left in your life. How will you best spend the one precious resource you have, which is your hours of living? Are they to be wasted away absorbed in television? Are they to be frittered away in the pursuit of superficial trivialities that might be wiped out in an instant through some tragic accident or disaster?

Every now and then you need to step back and ask yourself, "While I'm still healthy and have the opportunity to devote my energies to something larger than myself that is of importance to the world, even if my contribution might seem only a little, what should it be?" You need to become the architect of your deeds just as you need to become the architect of your thoughts.

This very moment you must ask yourself, "Who am I really and what do I stand for? What is the most significant and worthy goal I want for my life? What am I trying to realize as my best self? Am I satisfied with the plot of my life? Am I being or supporting the light that I want others to see? What do I want to accomplish with the time I have left?"

After you choose your ultimate purposes, the next steps involve associating with the people who will help you achieve your goals or finding a way to tread those steps on your own. Most people cannot achieve their goals by themselves but need to associate with others who can help them achieve what they want in life. From just yourself you move to associating with a larger group of people and then from strength in numbers you can create a greater impact on the world. Sometimes you can indeed make that impact just by yourself, but most people require the camaraderie of others. Confucianism says that an influence starts with the self and then moves onto involving greater numbers.

Confucian cultivation essentially entails improving yourself to improve the world. We strive to improve in order to do better by ourselves and our world. Working on yourself is therefore enough in life because sometimes that is all that you can do due to the lack of opportunities and resources. Never be ashamed that you don't have much to contribute. Only be ashamed that you don't cultivate yourself in life. People regularly become monks, nuns, priests, etc. who take on vows of poverty in order to cultivate, so there is no guilt or shame in not having money in order to perform charity and accumulate merit in that way. What is important in the world is that you cultivate your self-behavior.

All throughout life, from the Emperor down to the common man, everyone must cultivate mindfulness to help purify their mind and behavior and continually guide them on a path of merit. Do not worry about the results of your actions in the world. Only worry that you are doing this and the right thing. Hinduism rightly says to become indifferent to the results of your actions, but strive to bring about what is better. Your guideline throughout all activities should be as Mencius said, *"biyou shiyan"* which means "always work at self-cultivation."

The Confucian way is excellent because it offers a fusion of the highest aspirations with down-to-earth practical methods. It teaches you how to master unwanted mental activities, use your mind properly, rise above your natural animal tendencies, and live your life in a higher fashion.

This is what the spiritual road is all about. If in using its methods you don't reach the highest heights, you will still be able to look back and say you have improved yourself, your outcomes, and have dramatically progressed from where you started. If you get really good at this, and cultivate your internal energy, you may even become a sage.

People often wonder about the role that religion should play in the future but those following the Confucian way don't worry. Why? Because you spiritualize yourself through these very methods. You *divinize* yourself by subscribing to higher, loftier principles that ennoble yourself and improve society. This is the highest road of philosophy, science and religion. This is the spiritual path.

The Confucian path of self-cultivation is that you work to cultivate both your body (including its internal energy) and mind for you can and must spiritualize both. You must train to master both the automatic and rational thinking processes of your mind with the objective of purifying both so that your mind can be used as the wish-fulfilling gem that it is.

You must also train to gain control of both your physical body and its internal vital energy or Qi.

You must also train to master your outer behavioral conduct of word and deed, involving yourself in harmonious relationships that help others while working to accomplish anything else you want to achieve in life.

Whatever your status in life - whether of wealth or deprivation – you should strive to find a purpose *for* your life along with purposes *within* your life. Hitch yourself to a dream or vision bigger than yourself. Unfortunately, many people must live in a restrained or inhibited way because of constraints or obligations, but the ideal is to *live your work* because of its contribution or importance rather than *working to live*. You want to find something to do in life that is contributing to make the world a better place. You want to devote yourself to a higher ideal greater than yourself with the free resources you have.

What you want to work on in life is becoming a better person, family member, friend to others, and member of your community and country. You want to perfect yourself by mastering purity of thought and deed, recognizing that your only true possession is consciousness that must be perfected. You want to work on polishing your character and freeing your thought processes of unnecessary afflictions so that you are always involved in correct thinking, and you want to seek out, learn and employ the best models you know of for arriving at decisions, determinations and plans of action. You want to master your body and its energy, your emotional attitudes and your behavior in the world of men and accomplishments.

This path of perfection is the Confucian way.

ABOUT THE AUTHOR

William Bodri is the author of several books on business performance, health and self-help including:

- *Socrates and the Enlightenment Path*
- *Move Forward: Powerful Strategies for Creating Better Outcomes in Life*
- *Quick, Fast, Done: Simple Time Management Secrets from Some of History's Greatest Leaders*
- *Look Younger, Live Longer*
- *Sport Visualization for the Elite Athlete*
- *Visualization Power*
- *Nyasa Yoga*

The author can be contacted for speeches or interviews through wbodri@gmail.com.

Made in the USA
Monee, IL
30 July 2022

10589962R00105